INNER
SPACE

A Book of Hope for Busy People

ANTHEA CHURCH

Inner Space

Reprinted 2006

ISBN No: 1-886872-05-8

Published by Brahma Kumaris Information Services Ltd., in
association with Brahma Kumaris World Spiritual University
(UK) Registered Charity No. 269971.
Global Co-operation House, 65 Pound Lane,
London NW10 2HH, UK

Designed by BookDesign™, London
Printed by Power Digital Printing Co Ltd. Hong Kong

www.bkpublications.com
email: enquiries@bkpublications.com

www.bkwsu.org

INNER
SPACE

A Book of Hope for Busy People

ANTHEA CHURCH

BK PUBLICATIONS
an imprint of
BRAHMA KUMARIS INFORMATION SERVICES LTD.

IV

The author's words speak sensitively and openly of her path to a new awareness of being, including both her own experiences and those of her special companions on the journey. We are presented with the challenge to find our own inner space and, through the exploration of this new terrain, to create for ourselves a more peaceful and meaningful existence.

CONTENTS

FOREWORD

You would think it was easy, inner space... As my ninety-year-old cousin said to me with a baffled incredulity on her old face when I told her that to preserve my space I meditated: 'But darling, why not just go to sleep?' She has a point. Sleep rearranges and refreshes the mind. But what about dreams, what about restlessness, what about the cricked neck as you sleep in the wrong position? 'Well,' she would say, ' just stretch, go for a walk or - well, darling - go for a holiday...' Again, she has a point and in her life, that kind of short term remedy for mental congestion has been effective. But she is ninety and she has lived all her years in the country where the rhythms are slower. I doubt she has ever experienced the rush of the tube in the early morning, the constant ringing of phones, the bleep of the fax machine and possibly (I ask her forgiveness here) I doubt too she has ever ventured far into the tangles of the subconscious or the vast spaces of the spiritual. 'I don't believe in God,' she says, her hands folded solidly upon her tweed knees, 'and that is that.' 'Inner Space' is a diary. It is a record of steps I have taken to become quiet; steps I have constantly to repeat, for the journey I am on seems cyclical rather than linear. The book speaks to those people for whom, naggingly, quick fixes of relaxation - the holiday, the walk in the park, the drink with friends - are somehow not enough to answer the heart's cry for silence. It is for those in whom whispers the knowledge that quietness is not just to do with being relaxed and momentarily free of responsibility, but also to do with absolute honesty. It is also for those who believe in God but feel ambivalent about how to turn belief into experience, yet are willing to spend some time experimenting.

It is easy in the rush of life and the excitement of aspiration to forget those vague stirrings of curiosity about one's deeper self. One can live whole days in which one has, as it were, been away from home; away from oneself; and certainly, if there is a God, miles and miles from the subtle activities of that Being. This book says: 'Come close, sit down with yourself and have a look. Not just have a look, but look with love. Love, love, love.' Because unless we have love we cannot bear to look.

What will you find when you sit down and look? If you experience anything akin to what I have experienced in times of quietness, you will come to know that inner space is as simple as clearing out a room of junk; also as wrenching. For the photo on the wall holds memories, the clothes remind you of special occasions, the ornaments are connected with the people who gave them. That is, old ways of thinking are comfortable. They also provide credibility like a smart outfit or a good vocabulary.

Freedom is very bare compared to that. But it is also immensely exciting. And I have seen with my own eyes that anyone who has the courage to come very close to what lies behind the cluttering comforts of life becomes an exciting person. Calm yes, able to relax yes, mentally spacious yes, but also inspirational, because you never quite know what he is going to say next.

Making space inside is a delicate process. It has to be done carefully and supported by energies that are themselves already free of limitations. It is in that spirit that this book is written not in chapters but in steps. It is a book to walk, not just read!

It begins with a very condensed explanation of the spiritual framework within which I am working: the teachings of Raja Yoga. I put these at the beginning not to be dogmatic, but so that later references to aspects of those teachings will be familiar. And I write them in the style that they were told to me: personally, directly as if they were about me rather than just a set of abstract ideas.

THE PHILOSOPHY OF RAJA YOGA

You have a body; you are a soul. Infinitesimal, you move your body and you control your life. Leave your body and your body becomes inanimate. In you, the soul, is an intricate mechanism, the smooth working of which determines your life. In you, the soul, there is a mind which feels, an intellect which judges and assesses and a bank of memories which informs your feeling. Those memories come from many births. Some are good and some are not. Your quality as a person lies in your capacity to deal first with your feeling mind, second with your memories.

There is a God. He is a soul like you. He has no body, but He can use a body to work through. He has a mind that feels good things, an intellect that sees the whole picture of our human existence, and memories that are merely a record of His giving. Most importantly - and this is celebrated by all religions - He has no gender, because He is light; a point of pure energy that is totally free of the emotional traps that come of feeling oneself as man or woman. Throughout this book, I refer to God as 'He' simply because to use 'it' is in some way an insult and to put both 'He' and 'She' each time God is mentioned is to blur the very beautiful identity of that Being.

You have a task whether you want it or not. And that is to deal with your account of give and take. Everything you have done returns to you. If you are alert to that you can develop the strength to deal with it in a dignified unobtrusive way. If not, if you do not care about the quality of your activity, there may be a price to pay later. Everything you have ever done and ever said is recorded, and that is why you may feel sometimes, when meeting a person or going to a place, that you have seen them before. It is because you are linked with them. This is a very beautiful experience. It is also a challenge, like unravelling knots in a very long length of rope.

But God is there to help. God whose presence is felt here but who is not here; who has a home devoid of the push and pull of karma; a place of rest and complete silence in which nothing is done. You too have lived in that place once. You too have been without body, without commitments and without memories; in the wings, as it were, of this stage. The more, in moments of silence, you can recall that time, the faster you will reach the state of simplicity which is the destination of every human soul.

As well as God's world, there is above this one a subtle world; a quiet place, but where thinking, planning, supporting, inspiring happens. Call it the world of angels. People who see visions have touched this dimension. Finally there is here: the world of speech, action and interaction.

There are many religions. Even if you do not act upon or have feelings about a belief system, you belong either in a close or a very distant way to one. It may be a major religion or a small esoteric group. Together these religions form a tree. However much feelings of division and disagreement may suggest otherwise, all religions belong together because there is one trunk from which the branches spring and one Seed from which the tree grows. That Seed is God. When a person finds his place on that tree, be it Buddhist, Christian, Muslim or whatever, his life can proceed peacefully.

Your place might have shifted from birth to birth, for this is not your only life. You have lived in other countries, in other bodies; you have known what it is like to be both man and woman; and you have known a happier age than this one.

To recall that buried happiness you cannot live automatically. You have to take time to think deeply, be silent, explore your soul and deal with what you have become. For this there are rules which say: be careful where you go, how you spend your time, what you eat, how you speak. Just as a builder with a deadline focuses only on the unfinished house before him, once you decide to live spiritually, rules become merely a support to your concentration.

God is a part of this process. In His three forms as a Creator of wisdom, a Sustainer of all that is good and a Destroyer of evil, He looks after anyone who has this balance of caution and innocence.

These are the teachings of Raja Yoga. I was taught them in seven lessons when I was twenty-one years old. I can now explain them in ten minutes. But to live and enjoy their subtleties takes a lifetime; an extraordinarily rich and challenging lifetime.

INTRODUCTION

I am sitting on an Underground train. It is crowded. I look at everyone. I look at their faces, their clothes, what they are reading. I listen to their conversations and imagine their lives. I have constructed for the couple opposite a world of domestic tension, for the schoolchild beside me with his shorts, his plump knees, his well-packed school bag, a life of security: well-adjusted parents, picnics, holidays, homework.

Between these idle imaginings, the day threads itself brokenly: snatches of conversation, moments of tension, humour, confrontation. I think about tomorrow and when I shall get the time to photocopy different poems for each child in my class. And then my mind wanders into the more dangerous quagmire of self-questioning: why do you give them each a different poem, why not the same for all? 'But they are individuals.' 'But you will kill yourself one day if you go on like that.' 'Well, so be it. I'd rather die having served.'

By the time I reach my stop, my mind is so overcrowded it is almost unbearable. Blood rushes to my brain, possibly to deal with the burden, if that is what blood does! My legs feel weak. Maybe they are now without blood. And as for inner space, it feels in those moments as I place my bulging briefcase on the doormat, that it would take nothing short of a bulldozer to create it. Added to which, as I walk through the hallway, the phone rings...

A week later. Again on the tube. A man gets up and leaves a seat free. I sit down gently, with nothing more than a plastic carrier bag to manoeuvre. I left my briefcase at school. I look at no one, not because I am disciplined, but because they do not draw me. Instead I close my eyes. My eyelids feel soft against my eyes. My head feels calm. Is it imagination or does one's face expand into a broadness when one is relaxed? The day was good. So I can shed it easily like a garment that no one commented on because it was appropriate. I rest. Yes, above all, this drawing within is a rest. I do not try to think or not think anything. My mind just sits as passively as my body is positioned on the black and orange seat beside the door. This is not sleep but quietness and space. Space because things are in place. There are as many concerns, as many questions, hopes, shadows, lights, memories... But they are in place. Maybe they know that I will come to them. I will not neglect them and they are satisfied to stay for the time being filed, folded away.

My body does not move for the seven stations, though the train jolts mercilessly and for four minutes we stop in the darkness of a tunnel. But even that feels appropriate. A sense of no rush.

I walk slowly home from the station. Halfway there I think something I have never thought before. I think, 'I wonder if God has two sides. That is, I wonder if He or She or It (like I) has a job, a task, a commitment and then beyond that, a private existence which no one but the most finely attuned person can touch. I wonder if He lives a double life.' I enjoy this thought. It is like the agile twist of a dancer in the air. And air is the point, space. Last week that thought would have fragmented before it had even formed. And I think, 'I always want to be like this. I always want to be in this state where a dancer can appear suddenly on my stage.'

As I write, I imagine you. You are as busy as me. You too rush, fill your day too full, think too much. Or at least, very slightly, I hope you do, because then you will understand how crucial it is to know how to get from freneticism to peace. You will understand that it most often happens by accident. Some days just go that way. At the same time you will also know in the depths of you that there is more structure to those shifts than that.

This book is written in faith. It trusts that against all the odds of an overactive mind and an overcrowded life, one can find serenity. If one knows the way. And that there are landmarks as tangibly as there are stops on the Underground. The point is knowing the stops and wanting to get to the point of arrival, even if that arrival is a temporary resting place.

There are many ways to travel. Equally there are many ways to get from freneticism to peace. Some take more effort, more time and more soul-searching and cost money. In part as a defiance against society's complications, the strings it attaches, I have chosen what appears anyway to be the simple route: silence.

I would like to tell you something now that will be a test of that simplicity. I am going to write this book in eight weeks. Everything else I have written took months, sometimes years. This is deliberate. I know these eight weeks will be full, busy, overcrowded, without space. So, if despite that I can find stops on the way and note them down, maybe then I can say with quiet confidence that one can, without entering into the world of psychoanalysis, create this odd thing called inner space.

Having said that, you will also understand that this controlled experiment follows some years of research. It is not a sudden leap I make, although standing at the first step of the journey, it feels a little like that. I have thought for a long time about the mind and how to quieten it; nurture, strengthen, train it. But not just randomly. I chose a particular form of meditation and it is from the precious teachings called Raja Yoga, which are summarised on the preceding page, that these personal observations spring. I have placed them next to my life and tested my own integrity. That combination of theory and practice makes this a personal book. That is deliberate too. In the time that I have studied meditation, it has most often been people who have spoken personally who have awakened new insights. Their story has helped me unfold my own.

If you feel able, I would like you to try one thing. Keep this book with you for eight weeks. Walk beside me and see what you feel. If there is one thing I have learned and yet have still to keep learning day after day, it is that procrastination kills the spirit. If you want to change, however complicated you are, you have to do something bravely, simply, intensely for a set time and see what happens. Life will fight you all the way. It will say that you are busy, that this is all too generalised, that you have work to do... Don't listen. Eight weeks is nothing in a lifetime and always, always, there are snatches of time which can be used; newspaper, television, daydreaming times. Would you die if you did not read a newspaper for eight weeks? No. Please take that chance with me, because I promise you it is worth it.

In India they say: if you feel shadows cast upon you - 'bad omens' - meditate for one hour every day for a week and the omens will change. I have found that this works. And what are bad omens, but a sense of blurredness, a drudgery, a feeling of imprisonment within the mundane? It is to those who have reached their limit with the mundane and the constant chatter which the mundane provokes, that I hope this book speaks: through description, examples, instruction and strategies. All these will be there, because at different moments we need different poses.

Two last points. First, I have already mentioned God. If that has put you off, then close this book. It is not for you. It is impossible for me to pretend that this writing is anything other than an experiment with God. Without God, I would not dare even try it. Secondly, please do not be rankled by the instructive tone. When I write 'you', I am as much addressing myself as you. I am bossing, urging, encouraging myself. And yet that 'you' is my perception, in a quiet moment of 'you' in the plural. And for that reason, I wish you luck. Not the luck that wins you the lottery, but the luck that is in the hands of your love and your effort.

STEP ONE

DISCERNING

Why is it
that when you most need
your own love
you hit?
Even to ask that
is to add force
to your already raised hand.

Be gentle.
It is no sin
to be delicate.

Acceptance is the first step. Acceptance that there is something standing in the way of peace, that you are more often in the first frenetic state described in the introduction than the second calm one, but that does not mean you are a bad person. Oddly, for that really to sink in - that things are not quite right - you have to be feeling peaceful in the first place. You have for a moment to be calm. As such, acceptance is not only the first step but also the last.

It is that state in which you can stand before your own nature and not flinch; see what is blocking you and stay neutral. At the outset, the very act of looking is a challenge; at the end the challenge is to move beyond what you see and, in the moving beyond, watch everything change. For looking from above it is as though, free from your touch, problems dissolve on their own. More than anything, acceptance is being far, far from that state of hatred which springs most often from fear.

To reach acceptance, forget yourself and simply for a moment love the word. Love its connotations of kindness, generosity, openness and above all space. You would not strangle a crying child, you would give it loving space in which to recover or strengthen. Acceptance makes the face more beautiful, the body more relaxed. It brings into harmony all the people around you. It quietens the atmosphere, makes room for honesty.

Acceptance is a lovely word. And you have to want it very much. More than any material acquisition, you have for a few days to regard acceptance as the most precious thing in the world. Yes, it is just a word, but the word describes a quality and that quality exists as a resource in the universe to be tapped. It comes when you draw it to yourself by appreciating it. So in this opening period, turn it all ways in your mind. Look out for it in other people. Observe it in nature. I remember a poem by Thomas Hardy in which he talks about the trees which grow in the city: how the level of their acceptance is such that they never react as we might, against the fact that they cannot go on holiday, they cannot move an inch from their inappropriate and uncomfortable environment. They do not protest against the sweltering concrete; they just stand and accept. It is a dumb acceptance, but Hardy's poem conveys an enormous admiration.

Once you have loved the notion of acceptance, the journey begins.

Now I ask this quiet question. Why is it that I lack space inside? What is taking up all the room? What desire, hope, aspiration, feeling expands and multiplies inside so that even if I wanted to divert my attention from it, I could not? I leave the question unanswered. I let it sit and answer itself slowly, over a period of time.

Answers are most satisfying when they emerge not from the lips of astute friends or skilled professionals but from your own realising mind. I pretend as I write that I know you, but how can I know what you have built around yourself; how can I know the intricacies of your thought patterns which - might it not be so? - spring not just from responses to this life but to many other lives? Answers are private.

I think you have eventually to know the mechanism of your own soul: how it sabotages itself, how it excels. It is a good aim to have; to die not with the glazed eyes of a mind that has never examined itself, but with deep self-knowledge. The mistake is to be plunged into that process too soon by someone who does not have the full picture. And here, I would argue that only God is capable of giving that kind of training; a training which calls for intensity, periods of deep rest, celebration - each measured to exact proportions.

I have admired many people in my life. Often they have told me things I needed to know about myself, but I have tried my best never to make another person my oracle. To do that has always seemed an insult to life's way of shining through the eyes of strangers. And I have noticed that, focused on God, it is often strangers who speak, protect, warn as if their uninvolved hearts are the best medium for God to speak through.

So the question, why am I crowded out, has been asked and then left. Now be gentle. Do not probe, for that is tiring and when you lack inner space the thing you most need is rest and silence, not the stimulation of analysis.Of course it may be that when you read this, you think: 'But I have already walked a long way down the road of understanding myself.' It will therefore seem naive to discard your detailed self-knowledge and just be peaceful. It was easier for me. When I started to study meditation - which in its initial form is really a 'looking within' as described above - I was a very young twenty-one. I knew very little of the complications of myself. It was not hard to drink deep from a well of powerful thoughts. Only fifteen years later do I begin, with more spiritual muscle power, to face the particularities of myself.

If you have already done that kind of facing, the chances are that you will be weary in some way, and out of tune with the concept of a simple set of golden rules or in this case, eight steps to silence. I deeply understand that reserve. I also know that it is at the very moment when you least feel like the sparkle of simplicity, that you might most need it. Because to go on thinking, the brain needs strength. And strength comes from the nourishment of thoughts that are not constantly followed by qualifications; by ifs and buts and maybes.

Meditation is simple, because its focus is categorically on positivity. Any good teacher of meditation will know that the bulk of life is lived out in the grey area of uncertainty, but they will not reinforce that position of ambivalence. They will say: 'Come here, come and sit in this place, it is light.'

Having asked the question about what is taking away my space and then left it, I fall in love with the peace that I have felt at my quiet best; when silence has fallen, when my mind has finally hushed. Love, and come to recognise that beautiful calmness that springs from being centred. Know that feeling so well that you can invoke it at will. Know what it feels like in every limb of your body. Know that sense of every nerve, every muscle being in tune, your breath being slow, your face soft. Literally learn it, so that the moment you are away from it you know it.

Now I accept my specialness. All right, I may be getting life wrong. I may be ill, unhappy, in a muddle. But I know, as a mother knows of her crippled child, that I am special. Whatever has happened, there is a something that only I can do and only I can be. And it is the same for you. It is just a matter of discernment.

Here is a concept from the teachings of Raja Yoga which I use when I have lost touch with that self-respect. The teachings say that when you die, you reincarnate. They also say that a time comes when the process of reincarnation comes to a temporary halt. At that point, the soul leaves its last body and returns to the place of peace where it first began its existence. That place is like a rest home for souls. Previously, I used to wonder how one would know how to get there. Might I not end up, with my appalling sense of direction, on another planet somewhere, breathless on the edge of some crater? In silent moments, I have come to know that there is no danger of that. The soul will know where to go. It will magnetically be drawn back to a precise spot in the universe which is uniquely its own. There is absolutely no way, even though all souls have the same form, that it could at that moment ever gravitate to a spot that belongs to someone else. It is the power of your virtue that takes you to the right place, for virtue lifts you free of the pull of the planet. So never, never doubt your distinction. It is your right.

Nonetheless, specialness is often hidden under a lot of rubbish. Trust that. Sculpting makes dust, building makes rubble, painting makes smudges. All careful creating involves a lot of waste. This is the time for waste, because it is also the time for finding inside you the strength that has never left you, even in your more troubled incarnations. So do not hit yourself when you are not as you would like to be. In fact, when you are on the brink of change, you have to particularly admire yourself, as you might watching someone else honestly confront themselves.

Next, I trust time and also my own intelligence. I said this is the time to change. I know it so deeply that I do not need to explain it philosophically. I knew when I left university that this was a special time; that it was a time of change not just for me but for many other people. My own destiny was calling and there was nothing I could do about it. If it has not called you yet; if you think, 'Rubbish! Planetary impulses towards higher spiritual consciousness are a lot of New Age clap trap,' wait and see. One day, something will call you to a halt and you will know about it. If nothing happens (as it did not to me when I longed for a thunderbolt at my confirmation service and saw only the runny nose of the flu-ridden bishop; or an experience of sublimity during holy communion and instead just felt cold and restricted in my

green school uniform), well then it is just not the right time...
When I left university I went to live in a cottage in Devon. I
became a vegetarian and I worked in a library. I hardly spoke
for a year. I had been gregarious, but for that period I was
drawn into a kind of silence. People spoke to me, but
something about me repelled their intimacy. Even my parents
seemed like figures of the past. It was rather like communicating
through a soft, grey cloud. At the end of that year, I became
uncomfortable with this lifelessness. Only much later did I
see that after the philosophical and emotional discordancies
of Oxford, that year was a kind of digesting time. It cleared
my mind so that when my moment came, I could hear
clearly. Then all sorts of things happened. People gave me
books, strangers signalled, and eventually I found myself in
Edinburgh learning to meditate.

The point I am making is that we often do the right thing
without realising it. We are afraid, we are unsure, but an
intelligence deep inside guides us. And certainly when you are
to take a big step forward in your life, that intelligence already
knows. And quietly it begins to urge you into a
disengagement with superficiality, so that what used to rivet
you leaves you cold and you become ready to hear another
level of truth. Never be afraid of blurred times. They are like
recovery after illness or consolidation before promotion.

Learn to listen. Much of this book is about listening. And sometimes what you hear is: 'Not now. No, don't do anything now. You won't get it right if you do it now.' Have you a clothes catalogue? Look at it when you are tired and you will either indiscriminately want everything or you will want nothing. Look at it the next day when you are refreshed and you will pick out what would suit you. It could be a different catalogue completely for the two different ways you see it. Tiredness or bad timing make you see yourself wrongly.

Wait.... because inner space is not to do with a set of little strategies for mental efficiency - flowcharts, plans, speedy rearrangements of your timetable. It is about your heart, your feelings, your whole approach to life and most particularly your morality.

Lastly, trust God. Does it sound innocent? Like a child kneeling by the bed and saying: 'Bless mummy'? Well, in this context, the sense of being a child is a healthy one. It is, after all, what you are when you are learning anything new. And God is crucial, because if you really want to distance yourself from mental freneticism, find your peace, walk the right road - you need support. Friends, counsellors, relations will walk a long way with you, but they cannot always be close, nor can they always understand. It is my experience that God never ignores pleas from the heart.

This is what I do when I want to tell God something or when I want to calm down and find my peace. I do not pray. I sit quietly and in one sentence I say in my head what I conceive to be wrong with myself. And I extend that peacefully-held disorder upwards, like someone stretching their hand up to give something. Notice this makes me small and God tall. I, as it were, respectfully, not thinking this is a sin, place my thought in God's hand, and say, 'You take it.' It does not matter one bit at that moment about theology. It is a personal act that springs not from knowledge but from instinct, an absolute sense that He is there as an observing, caring presence. And that presence in this first expression of need is a maternal one. And my expression is a childlike one, a handing over of responsibility. For how do I know what life holds? How do I know who is the right person to tell, who to trust, where to go? In matters of deep, personal transformation, I am innocent; at this moment of setting out, I am tiny.

A good mother accepts. Even if you did not have a good mother, you will know that. Imagine it then (for somewhere in your existence will be a memory of skilled mothering) and, holding that image before God, watch Him respond.

God is not an old lady in the clouds any more than He is white-bearded and paternal. Of course not. He is good energy.   And that good energy is drawn to an accurate thought. Not only is it drawn by that thought, but it puts power into it, so that the thought becomes a feeling, an emotion, a sense of your own distinction and eventually an impulse to act. 'Yes,' suggest God's eyes, ' you may be as highly strung as a race horse, but you are also special and don't forget it.'

God is distinct, individual, but He has no body, no gender, no limitations; and His energy has to be attracted and activated through the human effort of creativity and trust. Be lazy, tell other people about your tangles, and in certain beautifully ruthless moods, you will notice that the emptiness you feel signals that God has withdrawn.

Remember this too. Every time you are brave, someone else is helped. When you become gentle with yourself, when you slow down and dance softly to life's music, all your relationships shift into a new key. You will stop pushing other people, you will relax your demands and they will bless you for that. So yes, this book is private, but do what it says and every single person in your life will be affected.

STEP TWO

LETTING GO

*To think
that the
heartbeat
of peace
could sound on
through my war...*

After ten years of academic study, satiated by critical theories, I ached for a guru. Even the word - strong, unequivocal - was attractive. I was sick of people saying: 'Of course you could look at it this way, but equally this.' Adults seemed afraid of certainty and instinct had no place in the serious acquisition of one's views on life.

Learning to meditate, I met no guru, but instead hit upon instruction that was unashamedly definitive without being superficial. I have come to love that instruction because it is humble. It is without the loud, sometimes deafening ring of a personal voice.

I return to it today because I know that it is the answer to congestion. It stands before me exactly as it did fifteen years ago and gently it calls: 'Have you forgotten me?'

It says: 'All right, you have commitments, you have a lot to do, but I should like to remind you that one day you will die. Are you ready for that or is your clothing so tight that at that moment, your departure will be an inelegant struggle out of too many layers?'

Does it hurt for a moment to conceive of yourself at that moment of aloneness; without family, without job, without friends? Maybe at first it does. Why? Because these things are an extension, like roots in soil, of our very being. They are full of us and we of them so that, small as our bodies may be, our emotional bodies are vast. They stretch into our workplace, into the psyches of all whom we love. To withdraw involvement is a deprivation on both sides. And yet initially, it is these very extensions of ourselves that create the noise in our heads.

In caring about our work, we unconsciously accumulate the concerns of everyone we are with. For it is not the activity itself that tires us. Mostly we sit, we write, we speak, we pick up the phone. But we are not alone. The air is full of the noise of discontent or excitement and it is this that we carry home like a layer of dust upon our clothes. And we like it, because when our ears ring with noise and our minds touch and entangle with other minds, we feel that we are alive; that we are achieving something. But also we are tired.

Then we go home and meet the responses of hearts that are so close they are a part of our own. The noise of caring is one of the loudest. Then there is money and health and buildings and furniture and a thousand things, so that even something as innocent as a table seems to call for attention, because it needs revarnishing and only you can do it. That is another loud noise: 'No one but me can do this job.' So it comes to a point when everywhere we look, a task calls, a mind asks, a hand requests.

What do I do then? I go for a walk, and that is nice, because trees ask for nothing, but it still takes half a mile of striding before I have forgotten the unvarnished table. And then I wish I could block my ears or be blessed with a tardis!

Or you may, as I was when I started to meditate, be at too great a distance from commitments, so that I stretched out and there was nothing, for what does an English graduate do with no money and an aversion to typing? Too much space is just as noisy as none. In fact it is worse, because it cannot even claim to be purposeful.

None of this is to disparage the mind that grabs so avidly for sensation. It is the most amazing instrument of experience. Its speed is stunning, its subtlety invaluable. In its capacity to work on so many levels at once, it is more sophisticated than the technology it has itself created. It is just that maybe, like everything else about our planet, it has become overloaded, overused, even abused. There is no hatred in my description of its franticness. I just see that sometimes it needs rest, a kind of relaxing preview of death. And that rest comes from the awakening of the uninvolved self.

Observe to where your thoughts go. Sit somewhere without obvious demands on your attention and watch. Then walk again. Can you fully enjoy the ridges of bark against your back as you sit under a tree, or are you still mentally with the unvarnished table? Do the thoughts come fast; do they, as it were, charge through your mind violently or file softly past? Yes, each time you look it will be different. That does not matter. The thing is that in the doing lies a birth. The birth of your observing self. And this book is full of births. Each is worth celebrating.

When something is born you look at it carefully. So look carefully at and attune yourself to this awakened observer. Who is it? Clearly, it is not any one of the thoughts you are having. Nor exactly is it what is having the thoughts. It feels more sensible, more far-reaching than that. Feel it as, if blind, you might pass your hands across the features of a face to sense what it looks like.

This is a crucial moment, for it is with this part of you that all the rest of the work is done. This part of you - let's call it the inner eye - is really your friend, because when developed, it can stand quite distinctly and operate on its own, apart from the rotation of thoughts.

Sit with this concept of the uninvolved self. It is a precious moment, for in it is the relief of space; a wider, more airy view. I am doing it now, for I too am still subject to the mistake that whatever I am feeling at this moment is the sum of who I am. This makes me dizzy, for too close to the swings and roundabout of moods, I become, as it were, a hundred different people in a day.

Maybe you will say: 'But this observer is not virginal. It is already old; it already has its way of looking: disdain for worry, admiration for courage. It knows what it thinks.' And this is true; it does. According to culture, background, belief system, occupation, so the eye will look. Never mind that. At least you have taken one step back from the part of you which moves like lightning; that is so connected to the senses that you have had ten thoughts about a face your physical eyes have merely glimpsed. At least you are out of that arena.

What then? Just stay with that inner eye, dogmatic and critical as it may be. It is the safest place to be for a person who wants to change, because it is the part of you that can learn. It has learned to believe certain things already and it can learn again. The mind which strains under the plethora of messages sent by the senses is not an easy faculty to educate. It is like trying to hold a fish in your hands. It slips and leaps.

In the observer seat, you question your life. You assess your mood, reflect upon your behaviour. And this type of thought draws you into a slower mode. It is a thought outside the arena of mere survival. It is where quality happens. It is also where a yearning for insight takes place. A sensitive inner eye will always be on the lookout for solutions, new ideas.

Regrettably, that inner eye also tends to close. When it closes, you return to that small, crowded area that is occupied by tasks. Some live permanently in that task-orientated mode. I imagine you do not. You move in and out of immediacy and reflection. And the reflection will take different forms. Sometimes religious, sometimes moral, sometimes personal, sometimes emotional. Sometimes it will be in the meeting of someone else's intelligence that you move into reflection. A person's words will catch your attention and it is as though, for a moment, your inner eye flashes and brightens, because it has glimpsed a truth to which it deeply relates. But then the tasks crowd in again and the inner eye glazes over.

Not only that. The truth to which the observing self is responsive itself seems to fluctuate. Opinions change; beliefs crumble. Things that struck you as profound last year might this year leave you unmoved. So that observing, thinking self, that is so precious because it is educable, is also ephemeral. It too, like the mind, is subject to influence. For years and years it can sing simply to the sound of someone else's tune. It is very rare to meet someone with perfect spiritual eyesight.

Given that, is there nothing that is stable and reliable?

What about your personality? People speak of you as a sound person, a kind person, a thoughtful person, sometimes selfish. Upon you, they stamp their judgement so that you stand not still, but rigid within the framework they have created for you. And you do it yourself. Again, with your own inner eye, you look and assess and think, 'I am a kind person', or 'I am over-complicated.' But will you always be?

There are those who say that we never change; we are what we are. I would lie down to die if I believed that were true, for I breathe the air of endeavour. As a school teacher, if I thought that, I would damage every child I met.

So, what does that leave you with? If you are not your thoughts, you are not what is thinking them, you are not what is judging them, you are not even exactly the person who acts upon them, what are you?

Close your eyes. Another birth. In the very, very quiet of a space that is temporarily rendered invalid: thought, action, even personality, you will see something else. Not see, but sense with a faculty as far from the eyes as the moon is from the earth... a pulse that is you. It beats gently, constantly, like the movement of waves, on and on; a spiritual heartbeat. And it is peaceful. It is stable. It is rhythmic. It is neutral, unblamable. It is as much behind the scream of a toddler as the whimper of someone dying. Call it the soul, even the soul of the soul - for is not thought, is not reflection, also a part of the soul?

This part is both extremely experienced and absolutely innocent. The moment you touch it, you become ageless, for it has moved through time undamaged. You may have been many different things in your life, believed many different theories, but always, always in the background has been this pulse of peace that has no idea of time. Attune with that and you stand absolutely in the present, for though it is eternal, unlike the rest of you, it has no record of what you have done. It just is.

It just is and you just are. Just are. Not thinking, hoping, regretting, even feeling. Just being.

Only in quietness and a place of comfort, where you are not called to act out the parts you have assigned yourself, can you find this pulse. It may be in a familiar place or, as with me, it may, at the outset, be somewhere which does not speak back to you with memories. The Australian outback; that is where I think I first heard this pulse of peace. Sitting by a river in a place whose name I did not even know, a mile from a sheep station. No one had been to that riverbank for days, weeks, maybe months; and because of that I had free passage to that place in myself that I had not visited either, for years, maybe even births.

There is a moment for this experience. And when you come to call it back, it may take time. Your clothing is tight and, as you move among your friends and family, they throw upon you other garments that are heavy with different styles, colours, shapes. Take them off. Gradually, gently. Dust may fly up in your face, for these layers are old and have accumulated dirt, and that dirt is felt as thoughts. Then the clothes themselves will feel heavy in your hands. You will not want to put them down, for they will seem, though inanimate, to have a life of their own that calls you. The mother's costume will call you to care, the employee's to finish the task, and, more subtly, the nice person that in reality is only another more deceptively elegant costume will urge you to be sociable. Here you need strength and a return to that moment of clarity with which you opened this book and said: 'I want to stop.'

Go on. Put them down. Lean your head back and listen, listen for that pulse. It is very, very quiet, but it is there. Beating on and on and on, oblivious. You cannot kill it even if a knife were plunged into your heart. Yes, at that moment your mind would leap in panic, your body would contort and buckle and maybe your reflective self might lurch out a question: 'Why me; what have I done to deserve this?' But that pulse would just go on beating. Beat, beat, beat as the soul lifted out of the body; beat, beat, beat, as it started its journey towards another body.

If it can withstand stabbing, then it can withstand the hundred other things that make you cry. Of course it can. It is strong, indestructible. That is a beautiful thought, isn't it! That however delicate and inadequate you may have thought yourself to be, there is this unbroken peace in the distance.

When you have heard it once, you can hear it again. And it is that constant return that will help you more than anything. Getting back to it is like clearing a road so that you can drive fast and easily. And if the road is blocked, fly! Seriously, this

hearing of the pulse is blissfully unrelated to the obvious ups
and downs of life. It is not conditional upon integrity
although it may be drowned out by the noise of tough times.
Even if you are tired, tense, taut, wired up, the fact is that the
pulse of peace is still beating. It is there, whenever, whatever.
Knowing that alone, you can reach it and breathe without sense
of your body, for that too will go one day. So don't analyse the
obstacles on the road; just get to the sea and breathe.

And once there, as nowhere else, you can relax. I am there
now. At this moment that my pen moves across the page, I
am far from the words it is forming. I am with that peace, for
in that state, activity carries on independent of the
momentum of will-power.

And it is here that, were my guru a physical person, I feel he
might smile because I have reached him and we would be
breathing together, standing before each other in the present
and yet completely alone with our own eternity. For no one
can touch this place in you. People may affect your mind;
they may influence the way you observe life; indeed, they
may help to shape your personality, but they cannot touch
this place. You can reach across to each other from here but
not touch. And that is a beautiful experience because, should
my guru say as he stands in peace: 'I should like you to stand

without moving, without even breathing, for three minutes', my response might be: 'Yes, why not?' because standing here, I have no memory of time, of pressure, of any difficulty at all.

If ever you want to achieve what seems impossible, what your mind fears, what your inner eye flashes out: 'Ridiculous!', stand here and you will be flooded with courage. Your breath will slow down and you will just do it. For it is the wrong use of breath which is most often the problem when we wish hard to do something.

Standing here, even matter begins to change. The greatest yogis I have met in India are right when they say: 'If ever you are ill, spend five minutes an hour in this position of peace and the very cells in your body can change.'

I am thinking of God now. What is He? He is a mind that loves; a mind that creates thoughts slowly and powerfully, not a single one wasted, like waves made far out to sea that eventually flatten gently on the shore of people's lives and soothe.

He is also an observer, and that observer sees the French Revolution as clearly and equally as it sees the tatters in the ozone layer; sees the future before it has happened, the past as if it were today, and all with an equanimity that comes of knowing the equal place of tragedy and joy.

And He has a personality. He acts. Not with a face, hands, legs but with appropriate thoughts that stretch out as tangibly and generously into receptive places as feet walk into a house. But behind all that, as with us, He too is a peace pulse. And His pulse of peace differs from ours in that it is much, much more powerful. While ours is very slightly vibrant, His is absolutely still. Ours holds steady our lives, His the universe.

And as I write, I remember my question about God's privacy. And the answer has come, maybe because I only asked once and I asked quietly. And it is this: that the most intimate life of God is lived out, as it is in ourselves, in this hidden pulse. If our miracles are played out from there, what can He do from there? Spin visions for the devoted...

The unvarnished table has gone now... It has no power over my flying mind. I got my tardis! It is the vehicle of thought.

I am resting.

STEP THREE

WITHDRAWING

I will sleep
at nine
if in the darkness
of the winter dawn
you will tell me
a secret

To keep attuned to that pulse of peace, you need to be comfortable. To be comfortable you have to take care of every part of you: your body, your skittish mind, your qualities as a person, your talents and most particularly your inner eye; your capacity for insight. Earlier, I said that it is with this quiet observing inner eye that all the work is done, for it is this that comes to know what is right and wrong. That knowledge then holds steady your immediate responses. If your inner eye is alert, then you are safe. If it is muddled you are vulnerable, because only your feelings are informing you.

This part of you can see very, very deeply if you wish it to. It can also see nothing - again, as you wish. If it sees deeply, stress cannot consume you, for your margins are wide. There is more space on the page than that filled by the fast scrawl of life. For a while you may be caught up by the visible, immediate demands, but you have somewhere to retreat to at the end of the day.

I have found that the best way to keep sharp the sight of my inner eye is to exercise it. You have to love to hide, to go to a quiet place and think. Then, at the expense of more obvious pleasures, you will receive rare and special gifts.

It is like reading. When you are absorbed in a good book, you have for a week or so another world to inhabit, a place in which to relax and be entertained. The trouble with fiction is that it is fiction. When the last page comes, the story is over and you are back with yourself and your immediacy. But stored within you is a whole library of books, a whole history. That does not go away at the end of a week. We read so much and yet we do not read these books which are ourselves. Why? Maybe because we do not love ourselves enough.

If you love someone you want to listen, watch, touch them fully. You are fascinated. So often we have this feeling about other people but not for ourselves. Why? Immediacy again. We are stuck with the ordinary self, the fast-moving moody self, so we don't want to look further. But there is so much beauty there if you care to look. It just depends where you focus. Look again and again at a broken button on a coat and you begin to hate the coat. But what of its silk lining, its beautifully tailored sleeves?

Regardless of their visible traits, anyone who picks up a book on meditation definitely has a beautiful self worth contemplating; a capacity to be touched by depth and breadth. Prisoners have loved to learn meditation. Why? Because it is generous. It does not confront you constantly with what is wrong, but says: 'Leave that; be deep; see beneath, above, beyond...' And that is not escapism, it is sustenance. For when you have tackled the intricacies of a deep concept, you can better handle the hard mashed potato and the violence of a prison canteen!

The main attribute of the inner eye is that it has seen many, many more things than your physical eyes. It has lived many lives; moved through different cultures and lands. It can, if you let it, open and widen to take in a much longer span of time than the twenty, forty, sixty years of your body. It has seen so much. Of course, it is natural to forget. If you remembered every life and knew of every one to come, you would probably go insane. And yet the sense of that eternity, with the occasional specific insight, is a healthy one, for it increases your stability. Along with the indestructibility of the beat of peace is also the indestructibility of your experience. You have been so far, seen so much.

I remember once, before I had ever thought seriously about reincarnation, being taken by a friend to visit a fellow student at Magdalen College, Oxford. I had never met him before. His room, unlike my own and those of my friends, was very sparse and immaculately tidy. On the wall were two or three Chinese prints. When he came out of his bedroom to meet us, I remember thinking that, although from Lancashire, he too looked Chinese. We had tea. I forgot this thought until half way through our meeting, almost cutting into it as an interruption from outside (although it was our inner selves moving in synchronicity to the surface), we became silent. We simply stopped talking and sat. The whole room began to resonate. That was the first time I acknowledged that silence has its own sound, its own quality. We must have sat like that, cocooned from the sounds in the quad below for at least ten minutes.   Afterwards, when we spoke, it was brief, profoundly respectful, like an exchange between monks, emerging from a session of silent chanting! What was absolutely clear was that we had met before.

That recognition made a space and silence in our day so vast that I remember it even now and it seemed (I don't think I am retrospectively embellishing it) to stretch into the days that followed and sustain what was to become a complicated and sometimes troubling triangular relationship.

Since then and particularly since meditating, there have been countless moments like that, where literally silence has fallen;

space has been made as a truth rises to the surface, absorbs and clears away that which is ordinary. I would say very sincerely that I live for those moments, because they emerge in me a love for myself so deep that I am able more naturally to love other people.

Four more. I describe them simply because they bring onto the page that atmosphere of wonder that exists at the margins of life. Afterwards I shall try and explain what I think brings these moments.

The first happened in India.

I am sitting in the meditation room that is situated at the heart of the Spiritual University which is the headquarters for all the Raja Yoga centres in the world. It is seven in the evening, Christmas time, cold. I am inelegantly buried under three or four jumpers and a blanket, initially with my eyes closed, trying to settle my frozen body. All day it had been hot, but now the sun has gone down, the cold begins to set in until the water freezes in the stone sinks we wash our plates in. I settle into a kind of inertia, begin to doze... Then suddenly I feel myself becoming, as if by the bidding of an invisible presence, very slightly excited. Something is going to happen. I sit bolt upright and wait. And it is as if at that moment, every concern, every question, every hope is silenced and I am nothing but the sum of that present moment; I, a soul, alert, waiting, listening. And upon that silence, like features of a face coming into focus, I see myself not as a young woman - flesh, blood - but as a being of light. I see myself at the time of death.

I am standing somewhere very high, and it is as if the whole world is sliding slowly past me. Every person in the world is a part of this vast procession that is moving fast and yet somehow with extraordinary grace and ease. They are slipping into another dimension that is far, far above where I am standing. And yet, before they reach there, they are each, in an individual yet intimate way, being healed. And that healing takes different forms according to whom they are standing in front of. When they come in front of me, I am clearly and absolutely aware of what I have to do. It is as clinical and yet caring as the work of a dentist removing gold from a tooth. I am, it seems, within seconds, or whatever measurement is appropriate, to see into them and lift to safety, from this position of emotional ruins, the special quality that they have carried through time. No, not lift, touch. And as I touch that point of uniqueness, they seem to light up as if it is their last hope; as if everything else has gone.

I must have sat with this scene passing across my inner eye for half an hour. I was not in a trance, nor was I dreaming, but I was unaware of the movement of bodies around me; the casual getting up and sitting down of people as they came to the meditation room for a few moments of silence. When I did get up, I walked to the dining room like a kindled lamp. I could feel my eyes full of light. Every cell of my body seemed vibrant and everyone I saw smiled, as if the experience were spilling into the air like stardust. That was almost ten years ago.

As with the first, this second experience made real what I had intellectually considered again and again: that there are many deaths; that each time we finish a life, we go through a consolidation, but that a moment comes when it is all over, when the soul leaves its last body and, temporarily at least, it rests; and that as it leaves for the last time, it is shown many things about itself: some painful, some beautiful, but all benevolent. In those moments, it is brought to a state of completion. It is forgiven, shown, taught, praised, cherished, loved. All in the space of seconds. And then it becomes silent. I believe that now, because I have seen it, but I do not think I would have seen it if I had not thought about it first. It was as if I had drawn the lines of a sketch and someone else was filling them with colour. It made me realise the tremendous value of contemplation. Even if that contemplation is a clumsy attempt at realisation, it keeps the inner eye receptive and fit so that when you least expect it - I was after all both freezing cold and half asleep! - you are shown something special.

What to think about?

Think of yourself as a soul that has lived through many lives; think of what follows death; think of the values that you cherish; think about the nature of God. But then be gentle, be humble. Think deeply but also be quiet, passive almost, for secrets are not attracted to a hyperactive mind, however intelligent. Be like the night sky: calm, solid, quiet, and one day a whole train of thought will alight upon your mind like a formation of stars. And when it happens, that upon your quietness a secret glimmers, you will notice that vast spaces are made in your routine, because the touch of one dimension upon another does strangely wonderful things to your commitments. It diminishes and lightens them so that they are no longer huge and solid before you. They continue to be important, but they neither move you nor take you so fast into a state of emotional involvement.

The third experience. It is somewhat to make the same point, that time made for contemplation on things other than practicalities is a spiritual investment. Again in India, I am sitting with a middle-aged Indian lady called Didi Manmohini. I cannot help staring at her eyes. They are glaringly bright, almost fierce and all her features combine subtlety with the kind of immense strength you sometimes see in the faces of Buddhist masters. I am afraid of her. I sense I have to be careful what I am thinking when I am with her; that she will know if my thoughts have moved outside the severe boundaries she draws up for her own thinking. I also trust her. She knows how to care for people in the deepest sense, not least because she knows when to withdraw. She sleeps early so that she can have a powerful meditation in the morning and so serve people more sensitively.

There are seventy or so of us in the room. We are sitting in rows while she conducts a meditation. I am somewhere near the back. About ten minutes into the meditation I feel myself focusing more carefully, sitting up straighter. I am alert. From a distance she has brushed up my thoughts and made me ready. I look at her face, her eyes and finally rest my gaze on her forehead. And very slowly there appears on that wide, smooth expanse of velvet brown skin the form of a star. I blink. I am cynical about visions. But this captures my attention. Its sparkle becomes so intense that her whole face is obscured.

I close my eyes. Then gently, I feel myself rising out of my body and she - her consciousness, that is - is rising alongside me, as if together we are flying far, far beyond. I have absolutely no physical sensation whatever. I might be totally without a body at all. It is a really lovely experience.

For a long time I had known and tried to feel that the soul and body were separate. I loved this idea, but as soon as I practised it, I became painfully aware of each one of my limbs as if, with that new acuteness, I could hear even more of the body than ever. I could hear the flow of the blood, the beat of the heart, even the pulse and it was all so loud there was no chance for profundity. It was like being underneath the roar of a waterfall. But in those few moments, maybe because I had tried and there was faith, I was shown what it means to be aware of the soul. More than that, in our dual flight, there was a wonderful feeling of togetherness. I knew then that there were many out-of-the-body tasks to be done and that they would not be done alone, but in formations of friends. And, although I had never really spoken to this lady before and shortly afterwards she died, I felt quite definitely that, dead or alive, she was my friend, and one day, somehow, somewhere, our souls would carry out a task together.

Again, what was sleep after that? What was dinner after that? What was the wrangle over who would carry the chairs into the hall after that? What was the mild discomfort in my foot after falling up the stairs later? Nothing: a game merely, to be enjoyed and forgotten. The experience totally rearranged my perception, made light of my life.

After that meditation, Didi leant forward and told us in a very soft voice that she had experienced something she had never felt before; that she was floating far, far beyond her body in the company of other sparkling stars. After she had spoken, she invited us up to meet her and to take gifts of sweets and fruit. My heart was pounding. I couldn't care less about the sweets and fruit, but I wanted to exclaim: 'Hey, that was me you were talking about; that was me you were flying with.' I did not speak, but my eyes shouted the words for me. She fairly slapped the sweets and fruit into my palm as though clapping a hand over my mouth. Meditational experiences come as investments for hard times. That is what her hand said: 'Be dignified, fold this experience to your heart.'

When I have these experiences, I feel valuable. It is like someone being in love with you, sweeping you away, showing you a special place that is of a different order completely from your day-to-day one. They are gifts from God and they come with a price.

There is a law that is as basic to the way of life in the East as water: the law of karma. And it says: every action has a reaction. I believe that, free as He is, God is not beyond this law; that He can only respond in a consistent way, in accordance with the effort that you make to free yourself from limited thinking. Principally, that effort to free yourself is to do with thinking consciously; as it were, exercising your inner eye to look more and more deeply, more and more broadly, more and more subtly. Stretch its looking to perceive the soul within the body, the world of souls beyond this world, the tasks that might be involved in laying each soul to rest, and the journey through time on which your soul has been. Giving time for this - even ten minutes daily - is like making time to improve your appearance to attract another person. Deep thought attracts the glance of God, so that suddenly amidst what must be a vast agenda of tasks, souls, concerns, constellations, His glance falls upon you. And it is like a kiss in which you do not lose but gain your purity.

The last experience I want to describe happened in a meditation centre in East London. It was an innocent scene, but to my inner eye it came as a wonderful shock.

The Chaplain of the school where I used to teach had come to lunch. He sat with his back to the sitting room window and gently we chatted. He had been at the school for over twenty years and was much respected and loved. Nonetheless I vaguely sensed a weariness in him. His voice had the same Northern briskness, and he kept firmly to the ground of trivia as usual, as if maybe I represented for him a subtlety, a lack of robustness that he slightly disliked.

Then the woman who runs the meditation centre brought in a little girl of about five. The child was both spontaneous and extremely purposeful. She went straight for the Chaplain and climbed onto his lap, as though to deliver a message. Tangibly, all she did was pinch his cheek and tell him he was her friend. As she touched him, my inner eye flashed. I was acutely aware that an exchange of a very subtle kind was taking place between them. It was as though for those few moments I was let into a secret of how invisible exchanges work. The child seemed to be carrying dispassionately, yet carefully held within her affection, a specific point of very pure energy. It was not her own energy, it was simply something she was carrying. As she touched the man, she was giving it to him. He was needing it. Not so much for himself but, I sensed, for a burden he might have to carry for others. He had a task to do and she was providing the energy for it to be accomplished. Six months later, I heard that he had left the school and been appointed Archdeacon of his Diocese.

Over the meal that followed that scene, I was animated. In glimpsing this event, I too was charged; and you cannot imagine energy. It is there or it is not. Further, I did not need to verify my perception. I saw, I experienced and then I forgot. In retrospect, that scene was a sequel to a lot of deep thought. I had contemplated for many hours on the way religions begin, progress, complicate, lose power. I had understood that for each religion there are turning points; that these come with the emergence of powerful individuals, and that those individuals are inspired. Each turning point I pictured as the shaping of a branch. Each religion having its different highlights, the branches all look different. I also pictured that they all drew on the same Seed, and that common to all of them were the processes of birth, growth, weakening and decay with the human body. That man sitting in the window was weakening. That child gave him strength. It was as simple as that.

Such experiences are crucial to a meditator, just as gifts are to a growing child: spaced out, given at exactly the right moment. And they come most especially when you lift yourself physically out of your normal environment, as a child might wear special clothes for an occasion. They follow imaginative stretch, and they fill you with the kind of joy that sweeps away burdens, like a lover placing flowers in your arms.

STEP FOUR

BEING PATIENT

I may be rough
when you are
caught in my currents
but seen from above
I am a gentle perfect curve
leading to the sea

The experiences of the inner eye - those times of sudden awareness when you realise the significance of an event - are the milestones of your life. They show you the way that moves through birth and death unbroken. In fact, as Sogyal Rinpoche says in his book on living and dying, they are often more pronounced in the period just after death, because at that time the consciousness is not protected by the body. Just after a person dies, the speed of their learning process intensifies enormously. It is then that they need most support. In life too, when a person is gifted with an intensity of insight, as well as being a support, they also need support. They should not have to worry about food and drink and clothing, for their depth makes inner space for all of us and we owe them for that.

But all of us receive gifts of insight from time to time and, though they may appear to come unbidden, they usually follow a period of consistent work. That work is no more than the effort to think at a deep level; and, sometimes more importantly, to think lovingly. I do not mean love as an emotion, a set of passionate preferences, for these too are potentially space-consuming, but love in its gentle form, a state which is indiscriminate, pervasive, peaceful.

There are many things in day-to-day life which challenge that level of calm love: in my case, crushed journeys to work, noisy classrooms, the clatter of tap dancers' feet above my head as I search for the right word, ailments, weaknesses, doubts... It takes very little to be steered into that state of force which is the total opposite of love.

Lovelessness or force is the enemy of depth and space. It creates the most noise of all and, like a systemic illness, it affects every part of your life until everything feels just out; just wrong. In that state, the inner eye closes, and those wonderful subtleties are gone.

Love is at the heart of space, because anything or anyone whom you really love will always stand aside for you. They will not crowd you out; they will not keep demanding, because the very state of love is such that it meets needs in a natural way. If you deal with people and tasks forcefully or too fast, however apparently thorough and generous you are, those tasks or those people will always shout out for more, like disrespected children who have been given junk food and react by becoming hyperactive.

When I feel love slipping from me - that ability to embrace life fully, slowly, taste it completely - I try to pause and calculate the damage I am doing. I see how I am hurting my body, other people; and, though I may be able to say I have 'done' a considerable number of tasks during the day, I ask myself how important they were; if they gave any pleasure other than that of ticking them off a list. I have come to recognise that living by a list is a form of anger. It is an anger with nature; an anger with the processes of life. It is like having wonderful clothes and never wanting to wear them because they will get dirty, or not wanting a situation to blossom in case it loses its power and turns into an unwieldy complication. Life is an unwieldy complication. It does not arrange itself into a formation of sequenced pages until it is biographised by someone else or subjected to the careful arrangement of an artist.

I think of my mother (who in her own way is an artist) as she daily used to cram saucepans into a cupboard, mumbling 'Get in there, you ruddy thing!' and it seemed to be more than saucepans she was reprimanding. Life itself was her target: for not being as she thought it ought to be. Another victim of perfectionism: a pupil of mine this week in a GCSE exam. She had beautiful handwriting, clear expression; she knew what to write but she could not find the right words.

Having formulated one perfectly intelligent sentence, she spent the next hour and three quarters crying and then finally ran out of the room. Next to her was another girl: racy, vigorous, careless, dyslexic; writing away, utterly oblivious of the fact that the poem she was analysing was not about a woman making apple crumble, but a man crumbling earth in his hands pondering on previous generations of farmers before him. The first girl, like my mother, found imperfection intolerable; the second found it fun.

Frustration can particularly be a problem for deep thinkers. We are striving for the stars but we cannot manage the saucepans! My answer to that is: forget the saucepans then. Go to the stars. In many instances, it is important to attend to physical detail first. You have to wake up, you have to dress, catch buses, earn your keep. If that is not going well, metaphysical speculation can seem an indulgence. But when the discontent stems from a more profound and innate unease with chaos, then personally I do look to perfection. I look to God for hope that perfection is possible; if not in my world, then somewhere in His. And I have found that, when my channels are open to that beauty, a lot of other more ordinary things, for being left untouched, fall into place on their own. As in the poem, the river does have its course if it is seen from above.

God. Maybe it is because I believe that He does embody perfection that I love Him so much. I used to love people who, from where I was standing, were much more advanced than myself; who knew more, had talents I lacked, were in their own way masters. I threw them out when they displayed their fallibility. I wanted them to be God. Only God is God, and only God has that elusive art that my pupils, my mother and I all struggle with: to combine a knowledge of brilliance with an acceptance of chaos. He does not try to arrange things, but He does, in my experience of meditation, help you to see the subtle patterns that make life exciting.

In His essential form, I understand God to be like the sun, warming in that indiscriminate way described above. His is love. Sometimes the vastness of that is too much to take in. Sometimes you can only experience it through the channelling and tangible presence of another person. That is especially so when you are stuck in a country where the sun does not shine; and there is the habit of subjecting yourself to harsh judgement.

One of the most important things I have learned is that, if I am treating myself badly, I am unable to feel God's love. In this He seems almost human. People who hate themselves are hard to love. Though in the most need, they are often the most obtuse, the most dismissive.

If you are like that to yourself, almost chemically, God cannot come close. I have met many people who think meditation, if described as an experience of union with God, is a nonsense. I have noticed that they are often very articulate, thoughtful people; people who have hurt themselves with their own intelligence or who have been hurt by someone else's. They do not like meditation because they do not like themselves.

It is crucial to like, and not just like - love - yourself. Sometimes, as I said, we need people to help us to that state. We need people with enormous patience who ignore our violence and keep on and on affirming our strengths. They are not those apparently kind people who elucidate our problems further, but those rare mother figures who focus again and again on what is beautiful in us. Such people are as precious as angels. Indeed they are angels, for what else is an angel but a being that links a person to God, in this case by easing your mind into a receptive, positive state?

There are a hundred arguments why we cannot do this for ourselves: our background, our demanding parents, our teachers, partners, life experiences. I would argue strongly that it is possible eventually to be our own angels. We only have to want to. And then, paradoxically of course, the right people come to help. So you are never really alone, if your aim is right.

When I started to meditate, I thought the first thing that would happen would be that I would spend a lot of time on my own thinking. Instead of that, I was instantly surrounded by people who were inviting me to use my talents. I was a drama teacher. They kept saying: 'Put a drama together; show us how it is done.' And from a distance, I think God supported and empowered their positive responses, for I doubt they could have been quite as angelic as they appeared. God was speaking through them.

I remember once showing a group of such people a short sketch that was to be performed the following week. I blush to remember it. The props were falling apart; no one knew their lines; the plot was so abstract as to be incomprehensible.

How was it then that they made me feel so talented, and yet also managed to cut the play from the programme? God must, I feel, have shaped their responses for them! For I did more and more theatre work after that; also talks, lectures, seminars. Some must have been frightful, but again there was this wonderful forward momentum. It did not matter. My skills, so undermined by a critical university culture, were returning like seedlings, sometimes fragile, but definitely green; definitely growing.

After that magical period, the real work began. And then it was - and still is - pleasurable to be made clearly aware of a weakness and yet feel as you might with a delicate chisel in your hand, standing before a sculpture. Usually it is a sledgehammer we hold. Once strengthened by love like a child, attending to chipped parts of ourselves is simply an extension of that process. And, standing on firm ground it becomes easier and easier to let someone else hold the chisel, for they may - not being the statue as well as the craftsman - have a better eye for the angle at which you should be touched. You have to know that, though your hands and feet might be wrong, your nose is perfect and that, with the sun falling upon that tiny part of your being, there is light enough for the renovation of the rest of yourself to be done accurately. You have to know your weak points, your vulnerabilities, your needs, your hopes very genuinely before the love can be distinct from arrogance.

The more evolved you are, the more active the self-study you are called to do. It requires a constant assessment of how you have behaved and the placing of that behaviour within a moral framework. For in that process is the beginning of honesty, of looking behind the words, the gestures, seeing yourself starkly until you get to the peace, the quiet, the eternal. But in seeing you are learning, and in learning you are loving, for you are not just bare peace; you are a thousand things besides and all in combination, making you distinct from the person next to you. Every bit of you is to be loved, even the dust that flies when the chisel slips.

The process of getting to know yourself takes time. It does not happen by a momentous unveiling. It is as complex as the cell structure in your body; and, though the structure is always there, there is a right moment for it to be seen. Those who give themselves up to a spiritual path, give themselves up to a sense of timing. They are helped by loving God and loving themselves, but also they will come to love and respect time. That timing might initially frustrate their own desires, saying: 'Never mind what you want; now is not the moment.' Love stops when you think the process of spiritual development is happening too slowly; when you want to hasten revelation. When you think you are ready. This is where love for the body comes in.

The body is honest. The body screams at deception. That scream is worth a lot because, as Edward Bach understood, it carries a message. When you hurry the process of self-knowledge or, conversely, when you block it, you make your body unhappy. It is matter; it has no consciousness, but its response is innocently intelligent and crucially informative. Walk it too fast and it aches; don't exercise it at all and it also aches. More subtly, resist your destiny and it tenses.

When the body is sending a strong message, don't lose your love. Listen and be grateful, for that patch of pain will remain in your mind later as a landmark. I had a headache for a whole year once. Every day I felt as if my head was going to split in two. There was a precise line of pain running from the centre of my forehead, right across the top of my skull and down the back of my neck. I got so mad with it that I would hit my head to try and relieve the pressure. Then gradually, I came to understand why it was that it was hurting. On a physical level there was a lack of minerals; spiritually I was unskilled in that little known art of being a telephone exchange for the thoughts and desperation of friends. My head was overloaded. Just as when someone keeps calling you, you finally shout impatiently: 'All right, I am coming!', so too in response to the cries of distress that somehow I was picking up from the minds of people with whom I was connected, I was shouting again and again: 'All right, all right, just wait!' And that 'Just wait!' or that 'Go away!' was like a negative mantra that had become so automatic it was hurting my head. It took a very special administering of love to put a space between myself and other people and to place in that space an atmosphere of peace, a pause. But it worked. And now I am grateful, because only now do I respect the fact that every single thought you have does something to the cells in your body. I had heard it a thousand times, but now I have lived it. It also made me love God more, because if I was suffering from knowing too much about sadness, what about God? What about the trillions of screams He must hear daily?

It is a great art to live correctly in the body, and it is wonderful to watch a person with that mastery. They may not have sophisticated clothes nor the obvious attributes of beauty, but there is a seatedness about their position in the body. Why? Space. They will tend not to be so much those who are constantly nurturing their bodies but those who have the art of leaving space between themselves and their skin. They have not just understood, but feel the truth of the fact that the body is a place of residence. It is not them. There will be a sense of lightness as if their features are illuminated. Their skin will be soft, for they have dignity that comes from not using something to the full. They are able to do with a little finger what someone else does with a whole hand.

In the teachings of Raja Yoga, it says: 'Learn to speak, walk, sit.' When I first heard that, I thought it sounded ridiculously basic, but I feel now there is a substantial amount to be learned about these three things. To speak with love is not just an emotional thing. It is physiological. It is the ability to put energy into your voice so that it stretches beyond the words; it is also to make all your words a message to yourself first. Then you are honest; you are filtering everything through your own system. Then people trust you. To sit in a dignified position is again not a matter of vanity. It is allowing the energy to move through the body easily. It is a matter of self-respect, of knowing your worth, of not identifying with the angular, lopsided emotions of other people in the room. It is being alone, keeping your clothes in order.

And as for walking, I always admired fast walkers; and yet when I think of myself in India - a place where I know I am most at peace - I recall that I walk slowly. It is as if my soul is moving my legs at the slow pace of its thought. My legs are being moved, and with each movement a wave of energy is passing down into the feet and into the ground. In London I walk fast. In that late, rushed walking is no love, no depth, no power and a speed that damages.

Speed kills love because it stops you seeing the patterns in things. You get up fast, you eat fast, you dress fast, you go to work fast, you speak fast, and at the end of the day you feel distressed or bored or restless. When you move slowly, you can hear the significance in life.

I have found that the most helpful way to steady my pace is to have a period of meditation in the early morning, for it is at this time that you can set the rhythm of your breath, your thoughts. And then automatically, though events might pressurise you, you are set to walk at the right speed. If you do not set yourself, life sets you. Then you feel seasick because the waves are so unpredictable.

Equally, I have found it useful to sit quietly for a few minutes before sleeping. The day, whatever it may have seemed superficially, is a treasure box. It is full of moments worth appreciating: the smile, the kind word, the bright colour, the spurt of energy, the moment of warmth. Always there is something. To focus for a few moments on those glimpses of goodness shifts the chemistry of your soul and body. It puts you into positive. Then you sleep better; you wake better. Then life plays you better cards, because an awareness of what is good invokes more good, as tangibly as in meditation self-respect invokes God.

Love, then, is to pay constant attention to yourself; to check that your thoughts are not damaging; to catch patterns of negativity before they become scars. This work is not a matter of power. It is habit. And if you are depressed, it may well be a chemical illness, a hormonal imbalance, a deficiency; but as much it is a negligence, a failing to attend to yourself daily.

If all that just seems too hard, begin by finding another person who has set themselves well. Last week I was at a meeting. We were to stop at twelve to make lunch and then resume at two. We all went into the kitchen and started making sandwiches. Within ten minutes I had made about fifteen. Out of the corner of my eye, I saw a large man with gentle hands mashing avocados in a bowl. He had, I reflected, been mashing for an incredibly long time. I looked at his face. His very features, his absorption and pleasure in this tiny task relaxed me. When the lunch was ready, I went straight for the avocado because of the gentleness he had put into its presentation. The food he had made had power.

And when the day seems to have been full of the equivalent of my shoddy sandwich-making, then it is useful to know how to shed it. As the natural health practitioners say: clean your aura. Shake out at the end of the day your dust. For it is not just your thoughts, but the thoughts of the people around you that create your mood. You feel unwell when their thoughts and yours have become mixed up and you cannot distinguish between them nor stop them. Then have a shower. Physically use water to clean them away. Only then will the good things stand out. Good things are like soap.

Lastly patience. If we have been born before, we have had many teachers. Anyone interested in meditation will be likely at some point to have sat before a master to learn to still their mind. It feels to me - and Raja Yoga stresses this - that this is a crucial time, for it is now that we can dismantle the negativity of many lives; not under the wisdom of any master - for what man could see the precise structure and form of all our births? - but under the wisdom of God. It is a big task. It is delicate. Often deeply concealed, invisible factors are dealt with. Sometimes you are not to understand the detail or you may, with the sharpness of your perception or the ruthlessness of your self-control, cut yourself. And sometimes you are to understand, and when that gift of insight comes, there is such joy.

Earlier this term, I took a sixth form group to see 'Measure for Measure', that play of Shakespeare's that deals, relevantly, with the perils of extremism and with the very inability just described to extract value from mediocrity. In the last scene, the heroine Isabella stands in court to defend herself in the presence of over a hundred male lawyers. On the vast stage she looked very small. I leant forward in my seat. Suddenly I was flooded with the most horrible fear that I was about to keel over on top of the lady sitting in the row in front of me. 'You must be tired,' I thought to myself. Then, literally at the moment when I felt I was going to pass out, a memory of having stood in such a situation myself rose to the surface of my mind. I knew without a single doubt that once, a long time ago, I had been frighteningly tried and accused in a law court. As the realisation rose to the surface, my space returned; I relaxed; I sat back in my seat. And I felt an amazing joy. Another piece in the jigsaw. Partly that revelation might have come as a reward for the troublesome task of booking seats, collecting money, shepherding students, making sure they did not snigger through long, incomprehensible speeches, and all that after a day's teaching. It was as though life was saying: 'You are attending to me fully, so I shall tell you a secret.'

When you do not know why you feel as you do and you have tried every strategy of positive thinking there is, then just wait; don't touch. This is the ultimate love and trust you can show for God the Teacher and also for yourself. A trust in which you do not ask to understand, but you wait to understand. It will come...

STEP FIVE

BEING BUSY

I protect not take
your space.
While you are with me
your heart, free of your own touch
heals in peace.

One of the biggest illusions is that to have space you need more time. You think: 'Don't give me that to do, that'll take more space.' Sometimes that is true; it will. As often it is not. It is thought that really takes the space, not action, and one of the most space-taking kinds of thought is thought about action.

There was an occasion once when a young woman in our mountain ashram in India had returned from a journey. She had spent three days in a train and was greatly relieved to get back to the quiet family atmosphere of the mountain top. Almost the moment she walked in, she was asked to pack her bags again and take another train because a job needed doing hundreds of miles away in another part of India. She was devastated. She had just arrived. She pleaded, she cried, but trained to obey, she went. Three days later she returned. In those three days, all those living in the ashram had received special experiences in meditation while she had been busy doing whatever it was she had been told to do. As she walked to her room, she met the head of the ashram. In a few seconds of contact with his light-filled eyes, she told us later, she had the equivalent experience of power and beauty that all the other sisters and brothers had taken three days to experience. It was a victory for action, also for trust.

In lesser ways I have experienced that myself. I have wanted to sleep. It has been late and someone has come to my room to talk. I have learned not to turn them away, because the quality of sleep that follows the settling of unrest, even if it is not your own, is always better. When you are sensitive, mental space can as easily be taken by other people's thoughts as by your own.

Nowadays I have come to consider action - which is really just a creative rather than withdrawing response to life - as liberating. You might be busy, but there is a rhythm to commitment as there never is to anticipation. Anticipation is full of nervous, uneven thought. Once you have involved yourself in action it is much easier to relax than if you have done nothing. Doing nothing can be one of the most tiring stances of all.

I need to tell myself this again and again, for inertia sometimes is still remarkably attractive. But I remember periods of unemployment before my teacher training course. Did I enjoy them; did I use them fully; what did I feel? If I am honest I would say I felt miserable. There was too much thought space; dangerous thought space, too much conversance with my own subconscious, possibly a few brushes with the subconscious of others too. I became heavy and confused. The moment I stepped into a classroom, that environment renowned for stress, I relaxed. There was no time to have thoughts that, in their unhealthy depth, only produce more thoughts.

And now all day is spent in the classroom. I am fully stretched, fully challenged and the evenings are precious, so precious, as they would not be if I had spent all day at home. Those few moments I spend in silence in the evening seem especially filled, as if someone is proud of my industry and wishes to pay tribute.

If you do not accept your business, if you hate it, your inner life perishes. It becomes a place of escape, a dream world which eventually, with no context in which to view it, has no power. Equally, when you are frightened of solitude, constantly inhabit activity and, as if you hate your own company, flank yourself purposely with people, then when you come to be alone you feel empty. I can think of no more blissful experience than that in which, busy at work, I have tender feelings about my solitude, and in solitude I look towards activity with enthusiasm. To refine that balance, which is itself the secret of quietness, is an art.

So which do you work on first: activity or quietness? To answer this I recall my first week of meditating. I was acting in a play in Edinburgh and taking meditation lessons during the day. At the end of my week's course, seeing no meaning in my proposed plan to do teacher training, I asked the meditation teacher if I could come with her to London. Sensing, with a wisdom I still love in her, my tendency towards what they call in India 'sanyas', (the forceful discarding of social responsibilities) she said without hesitation: 'No, go and do your teaching.' I was devastated. The world of work seemed utterly dry. What was it compared to the stillness, the depth, the sparkle I had seen in her eyes? It was nothing. But I followed her advice, and now I am so happy that I did. I am so happy that I am tested daily on the validity of my peace in the midst of a busy professional world.

Nonetheless, even after that I still needed some pushes and shoves to keep out there, to stay with people. So intensely that once I remember going to India feeling obscurely on the edge of death. There was nothing tangibly wrong, simply a feeling of utter neutrality towards all things and all people. I remember tidying my desk away at school as if to leave it ready for a successor, giving my car keys to a friend, even writing my will. I just felt I was going to die. In India I went to the wisest teacher I knew and told her. I was embarrassed. At twenty-eight, it sounded absurd. But she was calm. She said that she herself had felt about to die many times and that every time she had felt it she had been sent back. Literally sent, she said. As she spoke, music came through the speakers in her room. I was sitting beside her. As the music played and we became silent, she put her hand on my shoulder as if to ground me. Afterwards we spoke of other things. But I knew in those quiet moments something had happened.

The next term my teaching flourished. I felt a richness, a warmth, a love I had been utterly without in the preceding few months. In retrospect, I doubt she was aware of what had happened nor would she even remember the scene. But God would.

God in His role as a Father protects one from the abstract, the ghost world of self-absorption and gently steers one into crowded places. He also protects against the extremes of one's own personality, like a person standing at a cliff edge with arms outstretched. It happened again yesterday in a different way. I tell you because I want you to know how profoundly you are looked after if you try to walk any path honestly. That same woman who had nudged me back into involvement eight years ago met me again yesterday. I confess I was not excited about our meeting. Maybe it was because I had been so involved in marking exam papers that I felt distant from her. This time I had touched another extreme; I had over-involved myself in the world of activity. The magic of visions, of stars hovering on thought-free brows, of colourful images of past births were far, far away. I felt a little sad as if I had lost something, and I knew that seeing her would be like looking into a mirror and being faced with my own drabness. She said very little. Her feet were restless as if she too wanted to get away. For she is a little like God in the way she mirrors your own state back to you. Finally she asked me what I was writing. I think she barely heard my answer, but simply asked me what time of day I did my writing. As she spoke, she leant forward as though that question were of sudden importance. She was concerned that I should get my timing right. And seeing my closed state, my fear of reprimand perhaps, she simply said: 'Well, just don't rush it or you won't enjoy it.' Her words were clean, deep, clear. I knew she was right: that if in activity, rushing is dangerous; makes one thin, pale, insubstantial, meaningless; then manically goal-orientated activity makes one sad in a different way - homesick for depth - so that, seeing someone else's silent, richly absorbed face, one feels like stretching out a hand and saying: 'Take me with you, I want to be where you are'.

If someone were to ask me which should be the priority, work or quietness, reluctantly I would always answer work. Work comes first. You cannot fly where there is no ground to return to. And what is ground but the solid, simple hours of effort you put into being with people creatively, whatever your job? So forget space, first fill up. Be busy, even if that business is apparently mindless or tedious. Even if it is cleaning merely, or working in a garden or exercising. There must be a routine as there must be notes in music. And yet the magic is in the poised raising of the baton.

Activity and silence belong together. One cannot be right if the other is wrong. Right activity might seem simple, but it is not always so. It may look to everyone else that what you are doing is right, but it may not be if your motivation is wrong. Equally it may look as though you are doing very little, but if your thoughts are moving in the right direction, if your pausing is not laziness but merely a stretching out to quality, a refusal to continue 'doing' mindlessly, then you could well be right to do less. Even action is really to do with thought.

One thing I am now clear about is this. You cannot experience inner space if what you are doing is against the grain of your soul. If you are even a slightly good person, your mind will cry out if you are walking the wrong road. You may be able to laugh, to be good company, to get through your list of tasks efficiently, even have a relationship with relative success, but if you were to sit down and try and be silent, it would be impossible. Inner space is a moral thing. Love may be unconditional - although in reality I doubt that it ever is - but space is not. You have to accept that you are ultimately ruled by your conscience. You do not have to think what is wrong and what is right, your conscience already knows. And if your mind is unaccepting of its messages, your conscience will speak through your body instead. Although I love those roundly-spoken American tapes about the inner child, about total acceptance, in my heart I question their validity, because I just don't think it is possible to be unconditionally at peace. If something is wrong, it will scream at you until it is faced. A single step will do; an acknowledgement, the beginnings of a reconciliation, a gesture, but the healing must be initiated before you can rest.

What kind of activity produces those messages that ruin your silence? When I look back on stressful times, I realise that what I had been doing was based on some kind of negative energy. The Christians say there are seven deadly sins; the Buddhists say there are six. In Raja Yoga we speak of the five vices: attachment, ego, anger, greed and lust. If what you are doing has its roots in any of these, there is no chance of that deep quietness where every part of you – mind, body, heart, soul – are at rest. I think of Shakespeare again. He knew this so well. Almost every soliloquy spoken by his tragic heroes takes its length from the fact that its speaker is riddled with the doubt that comes from acting out of vice. His characters are heroes because they know they are walking the wrong road; they are tragic because they cannot extricate themselves.

Each vice has a different feel and each makes a different noise in the mind. And it is worth getting to know those feelings and sounds so that you can recognise them before they take too firm a grip. Knowledge is the first ingredient in any rescue remedy.

Attachment. Attachment is a long unbroken whine. It is a scream for attention, a demand for support, a completely unrealistic expectation of yourself and of other people, particularly those close to you. It is an unhealthy determination, and it creates thoughts such as: 'I'll do it whatever', 'I know this is right', 'I must do it now', 'But why doesn't anyone help me?' It is a noise which gets not just on your nerves but on everyone else's; it makes you restless and them irritable because you cannot leave things alone. You keep making phone calls, you rush people into things, you pressurise. The results may be immediately successful, but they are short-lived and may have a price, a complication in the relationship, for instance, between you and the person you have pushed into helping you. One day, when you wish to be quiet, they will come and demand payment in the form of your attention.

Place next to attachment ego. Ego is like the low heavy beat of drums. The beating upon one's chest: 'I am here; look at me.' It is the complete opposite of that invisible, tiny and very sweet beat of peace that has to be loved to be heard. Ego is one's most public self; that self which has a name, a form, a job, a culture, and which wishes always to be thought of primarily in that context. Ego makes everyone tired, for it goes on and on about itself. And the action that supports it is flamboyant, often very attractive, but also short-lived. It is action that is always done in public.

The noise of anger is deafening. It is a burst from the cymbals, then silence, then another burst. It says: 'That's not fair; that's just so unfair'. It is born out of ego; it follows the drums. It says, 'I did this and you never thanked; I did, I did, I did!' And all the small injustices of life rally before you in support of your case. Anger is the noise made by self-justification. The action that supports anger is literally so noisy no one can rest. Doors slam, keys drop, feet pound. If you have any sense, you will keep away from a person with anger, which is sad for they may well be crowded out themselves and wanting to be loved.

Greed is more gentle. It is that soft constant outstretch of the hands, that pulling towards oneself more protection against nakedness. It is the flute, very enticing, soothing, lilting, but pouring on and on for you have one thing, then you want something more and more and more until you are so protected that life ceases to excite you. Action based on greed is compulsive and restless.

And lust. Another soft instrument. Relaxing and yet blurring. It is when you lose the contours of your own being and feel merged with other people. It is at the heart of fashion, of copying, of going with the crowd. It kills originality. So its sound is muffled, indistinct, like the emperor in the story of 'The Emperor's New Clothes', who was fooled by fashion, and the only voice that could break the spell was the piping, pure voice of a child. Lust casts a spell on you so that you cannot think for yourself.

Possibly the noisiest of all, a broad term for all vices combined, is desire. When you want something with all your heart, you will never rest. Does that make you sad? Does that make you feel that the universe applauds blandness? There are moments when I feel this. Standing on the escalator, watching the slow procession of success stories advertised on billboards, I feel sad, for that road is not mine. Maybe it would be nice to be important, to be advertised and successful, but embedded in my heart is the knowledge that it is not the time for that. I have lived many times and in other births maybe I had my moment of glory. But I feel, and this feeling is corroborated by the teachings of Raja Yoga, that the drama, to use Shakespeare's term for life, is coming to a close. And when something is finishing, personal glorification, single-minded brilliance, loses its shine; it is too late for that. If it does come, it comes as riches to be shared or it comes simply so that the angle of people's vision is poised towards an energy that will help them.

I think of my school, a place where everyone is striving so hard for fame - it is a dance school. To succeed in that school you have constantly to shine, to have that ephemeral attractiveness which turns people's eyes. Yet when I think of the building, the place that my mind goes to most often is the coffee bar situated in the basement. It is run by two young men who have no more aspirations in their working life than to serve well-made sandwiches and fresh coffee. They have a special quality which stands out in stark contrast to the ambition of every other person in that building. The whole feeling they communicate in their patient assembling of tomatoes and cucumber is of peace and quiet. And I have noticed that the more ambitious people become, the more dangerously single-minded and desperate, the more peaceful these two young men seem to be. It is as if God has whispered in their ears and said: 'Provide an oasis in this desert of ambition.'

In two weeks' time we have our summer show. Everywhere there are rehearsals, there is stress, there are deadlines; and each day as I pass through the coffee bar, I see a different notice pinned to the counter. Yesterday the notice said: 'It is nice to be important, but it is more important to be nice.' These two young men strike me as the ones in our midst who have best understood success in its profoundest sense.

They do and ask for no reward but the right change across the counter. That brings space. To do and be prepared not just to see no tangible results but sometimes even to see your work dismantled - that is one of the greatest attributes a person can have. The sermoniser of the Gita understood that. So did Buddha. When the Buddhists speak of impermanence, my soul fills with peace. When they speak of the beautiful sand designs on a Tibetan monastery floor that are left to be blown away by the wind, I feel such pride. And yet I feel also that, though gone within seconds, they are also in some way, somewhere beyond perhaps, stored.

So what of space? The price for space is high. Money cannot buy it; time cannot bring it. Right action can. And you will always know if you have gone wrong. You will know because you will feel uncomfortable. You will not be able to look people in the eye. You will have secrets that separate you from people or you will have illness. And if you have been walking the wrong road for a long time, you will not have picked up this book, because you will not want to know. And if you are on the right road, what of space then? First of all, it will be easy because right action leads naturally to calmness, just as right thought leads easily into silence. All you need when you are walking the right road is to be determined and to be sensitive. You have to be sensitive to the way the road twists and turns as well as to the other traffic. You have to develop that sixth sense that knows that, however monumental your effort, at certain times even if you were to slam your foot on the accelerator, you would get nowhere. You have to sense hold-ups before they come. You have to know when words will fall on deaf ears, to be aware of which way the wind is blowing. It is a delicate matter, but it is a sensitivity not confined to psychics. It is the gift of any quietly observing person.

A way to develop this ability is purposely to create stops for quietness. Consciously decide that at certain times in the day you will withdraw. It is in these strategically placed pauses that you can, by being still, learn to read atmospheres. In the quiet of withdrawal, you can feel if there is upheaval or calm. Without knowing precisely what people are thinking, you can, as you become aware of your own thoughts, sense what other people are feeling. You can sense the vibrations of the place in which you are working. And in that knowledge comes the power of detachment. For when you know, you relax.

As meditators, we have been trained to stop regularly throughout the day for two or three minutes. At those times, we put down our pens, we stop what we are doing and we check ourselves. We try to stop even when the wind is behind us and the road is clear because that practice of stopping, when you in fact want to go on, is the practice that makes you the strongest. Why? Because it is symbolic; it is symbolic of drawing the line at desire. It is easy to stop when you have finished something, but to be able to stop mid-flow is a sign of real strength.

To flourish in any authoritative role, that capacity is vital. To be able to have someone knocking at your door just when a thought is forming, an idea emerging, and at that moment to be completely quiet and listen with total attention, is a wonderful gift.

What do you do with your mind in those three minutes when you stop? If activity has such a pull on the mind, if it is calling you so loudly, then the quietness of your inner world has to be just as powerful. That power can only be built slowly, and what is it built with? It is built with deep thoughts. One deep thought can bring such pleasure that it distances the hold of the external completely. It diminishes the weight of activity and makes it seem nothing.

What is a deep thought? A deep thought is a piece of information that comes to you as you stand on the line between the inner and the outer world. A deep thought is an insight into exactly what is happening in this scene in which you have been acting. It is when you stop, become quiet, withdraw your expectations and, seeing more clearly, you realise significance.

A deep thought can only come when there is the stillness of a framework through which you view your life. For instance, the law of karma is a framework. It is a way of seeing life to know that actions return to you as accurately as the tide turns. If that law of karma is in place in your mind, if too in place is the law that that karma has stretched through many births, then you will be blessed now and then with deep thoughts. You will act, and then when you stop to observe you will see behind the scenes. You will suddenly see why, for example, because in past births you have always been close to art, now, as you stand before a gallery of sculptures made of toothpaste tubes and mops, you feel like crying. You are not lightly offended but deeply upset by deterioration. The knowledge of the origin of that upset brings joy. You can tolerate anything because you understand.

It is the same with people. A present connection may be as simple as that between shopkeeper and customer, but it might, if you have met in another birth, be a lot more involved than that. When reincarnation ceases to be a theory and becomes a part of your heart, then it serves your understanding of many strange and immensely rich experiences. It also brings thoughts that are so deep your eyes shine. If you ever hanker after beauty, love deep thinking and all your features will change. I have seen this happen in a room full of meditators. When they begin, they look heavy and solid. All you can see are their physical features, their clothes, the expression on their faces. Then one of them has an idea; and that idea appears in his eyes as light, and you feel drawn to look at him, because he is generating an atmosphere. Then someone else has a powerful idea and his eyes light up too. On a good day, a room full of meditators is like a church full of lit candles.

And I would bet that, rising from that silent pose of inspiration, their very next action - whether it be to speak, to write, to study - would have been successful, carried as they were by an energy, a moral force. Their silence was full and so their action was right.

STEP SIX

BEING BRAVE

Would you
shatter
a crystal
held in your palm?

Never

Neither me then.

Serious people try hard. Their consciences are full scale orchestras that won't let them rest free of charge. They plan, aim, aspire; and then life comes along with its beautiful defiant force and blows the equivalent of their Tibetan sand picture completely away.

My headmistress at school. Lovingly, tirelessly, every week or so, she buys a new notebook and writes lists in it. By the end of the week, the notebook is stuck diagonally and dog-eared behind the filing cabinet. And in her hand is a scrap of paper. A scrap is better, for life - in our school, anyway - does not lend itself to the beauty of rose-decorated note books. It is a life full of scraps. Then she stamps and steams and generates noise; although to her credit, she always finally laughs as she discovers for the thousandth time that life is not as a child might be, asleep in her arms, soft-cheeked and quiet.

You are thwarted from finding your space if you try and turn life into your cherished child. It is not. It is an unwieldy, lumpy teenager, always complaining. And yet that impulse to embrace something quiet, something restful, is a good one and itself creates a state of inner space. I have noticed that, when I feel peaceless and crowded out, I can always be brought to stillness by the questioning face of someone needing help. If there is a genuine need, then power arises inside me, flooding out my own restlessness, and in touching the person in front of me, it is not only that one who is mothered but myself.

If you want to stay spacious, do not make life sweet and innocent, but think of your mind in that way. Think with the part of you that is becoming strong by deep thought, strong by silent pauses, that your mind is begging to be cherished. In the act of stretching out to your own mind, you will open and relax. And that mind is not just a child but a baby: a tiny, helpless, uncontrolled infant (the American therapists are right in this case) who is so volatile it is lovable one moment, the next, distressed.

Imagine you are carrying this infant constantly in your arms, and you will remain one step, one peaceful, inoffensive step, apart from the situation that you are in.

I remember having to make a farewell speech at my last school. I was terrified. The audience was large, critical and eagle-eyed. The speech was to be made at the end of a hefty luncheon, held in the octagonal school hall around which ran a balcony. I ate and drank nothing; my stomach turned. Just before I had to speak, I saw on the balcony the Maths teacher, usually as efficient and closed as a computer, rocking his child in his arms. His face looked different; his whole stance more relaxed. But more than that, I could see that compared to the exchange between him and his child, my speech which had kept me awake most of the night, was nothing. It was merely a few words scattered in the air and forgotten.

The vision of that man relaxed me. It made me, in those few seconds, realise that I too was carrying a child who was much, much more precious than the impact of my speech. It was much more important for my mind to remain calm and undamaged than for me to impress. I did a mental somersault and landed gently in a different space in which I was rocking my own child, urging it into quiet, for it had been screaming. As I stood up to speak I saw no one but myself.

It was not a particularly good speech; it was too long, too detailed, at moments hitting the wrong note, but beneath it lay a peace that lasted after the words. It made me promise myself that always I would care for my mind first, not other people. And it showed me that if I ever did want to help people, it could only be done like that - initially as a service to myself. Extending words that bypassed the cells of my body, I came to see that that would be hypocrisy. Maybe that is why my wise old meditation teacher became so intense when she advised me to write slowly: 'Write slowly or you won't enjoy it.' What she was really saying was: live the words, do not simply write them.

The image of the child is not just a metaphor; it is a fact that you are a double person: one who has nightmares, sees hideous faces in the dark, also picks up anything indiscriminately (feelings, moods, atmospheres) - like my nephew who brought in handfuls of earth from the garden thinking it was chocolate because it looked the same! Yet you are also the one who stands up in a suit and eloquently speaks - the adult to an audience of adults. If you do not nurture that child, then at some point or another, when you are dearly looking for space, it will thwart you. When my mind is rushing in a way that makes it a nuisance, I use my imagination. I picture my mind as a minuscule light in the centre of my forehead - just touching and glimmering on the surface of my skin. I feel it there like a flame in a lamp, and that thought makes me want to keep it kindled. To cup my hand (and that hand is a thought) around it and keep it alight makes me gentle, for it is like carrying something precious on your person and knowing that it won't be safe if you move too fast or awkwardly. It is also like walking with books on your head to stay straight-backed. Yet there is no heaviness in this sense of carrying a flame on your forehead. The soul is so light.

At other times I try and picture God and think: 'You look like that too. You are a light as well.' I imagine what I would have to be like to carry safely Your beauty upon my forehead. How steady, how quiet. At that moment I invoke God as a Child: innocent, because He has never had bad thoughts; light, because He carries no burden of regret. Innocent God. Very, very light God. And I think: 'What would I give You if You were to stay with me happily? Which thought would make the environment of my forehead comfortable for You? To feel You as a Mother I have become trusting; have handed over my burdens. To feel You as a Guru I have listened over and over to the beat of peace and tuned that beat to Yours. As an intimate Companion I have taken myself to special places, commitment-free places and prepared myself for surprises. To know You as a Teacher, I have learned not to hate the day; and as Father I have let You steer me towards action, checking it is always with the right motive. And now as a Child, a kind of Prince, I wonder if it is not my turn to protect You. To give You only good thoughts even if we are in a bad place.'

This reverence for one's own mind and its sensitivity, and more powerfully for God's mind, is a key to keeping a space between you and the world. It is a key to the quality of purity which is not prudishness but a freedom to be yourself, rather than be shaped as others would wish.

For that to work, to keep that space, you do need that quality most dear to children which is imagination. You need to be able to play with spiritual teachings until they become refined and beautiful enough to occupy you deeply. Chunks of theory are no good. Neither your own mind nor the mind of God is attracted to what is unrefined, any more than fast food served up as a meal would be welcomed by royalty.

Imagination is the capacity to assemble ideas in formation and make of them something new. In Raja Yoga we call this 'churning', though I think even that is a mundane term for the artistic activity this really is. Here is an example. It is the morning meditation class. There are two hundred of us in the room: people from all over London as well as a group from Holland.

Most of them are sitting on seats; some are happier with the floor. I am amongst the shoes. The person who is reading begins. She is reading an extract from a Raja Yoga teaching first given in the early seventies. In the Hindi language this is known as a 'murli'. 'Murli' means magic flute, and this metaphor is so right. To hear its sweet tune, you have to be very, very quiet and settled in yourself. Sometimes that tune disguises itself behind forceful, peremptory language. But the feeling behind it is never anything but soft.

It is hot in the room this morning. The shoes are distracting as is the occasional laughter, the jostling of minds trying to settle themselves, so I shut my eyes for a moment and say to myself: 'All day you will be marking exam papers; all day you will be confronted by repetition, by carelessness. These few moments are precious. All you have to do is sit, listen and be fed.' And being read to is so sweet. It is the basis for that most healthy consciousness that you are, from God's point of view, a child. So I become calm. I put aside other things, become oblivious even to the room. Occasionally, as I take off on a word or phrase, I seem to catch the eye of someone else flying in the same sky, and in those looks are brotherhood feelings of the most intimate kind.

The teaching goes something like this: 'If you have every relationship with God, you have so many different attainments. In each relationship there is a different attainment and, when all these are yours, it is easy to break your attachment to other things and to conquer your desires.

Remember God constantly and you will become full of power.' At first the words are general, informative, in effect merely equations; the details of the philosophy of karma: that if you do this, this will happen. Then I remember my book about inner space and how at the heart of each chapter lies a different relationship with God; that for a person to be full and content enough to withstand the noisy invasions of their own subconscious or the subconscious of others, they need a God of many faces. Faces which can magically clear away the wastage. And suddenly, as she reads, the words become music; they become mine. They seem, as it were, personally addressed, designed for today; not for yesterday but for today, now as I sit amidst the shoes. That makes me calm.

Then there is another passage. It is humorous. It describes how, when people talk to God, they are like shoppers in queues; they come for different things: some to complain, some to beg, some even to have their fortune told, but there are some - a handful only - who do not struggle when they sit before God, but instantly, quietly, as though dialling a direct line, can hear His voice. In one second they celebrate a meeting and that is because of their love.

Those words make different music in my mind. They make me deeply yearn, clearly and quietly. I knew at that moment what I wanted. The concept of queues before God seems the epitome of noise in all its indignity. The quiet, passive, faithful pose in which you trust God is intensely attractive to me. It creates a mental image, and that image is powerful, drawing to a stillness the thousand other poses I adopt during the day: chatting, requesting, asking, gossiping, discussing, desiring. It silences them all and becomes my aim, my calling.

I tell you this because I think it is crucial to have this live input daily. You cannot survive merely on your own energy. We each have different ways of getting this input. We go to the arts, to film, to sport... But of all - and I too love art and also sport; they are refreshing - the quiet, regular listening to spiritual teachings is the sweetest, for it reaches your deepest self and lights up forgotten memories. When a truth is lit up, you feel energised and defended. You feel you can look the day in the face.

I have since marked thirty exam papers today. It was easy. It has not been easy every day. So why today? I think it is because the feeling I had when I listened this morning converted itself into energy. Teachings properly heard do not retain their verbal form, do not sing uselessly in your head, but melt and transform into what you need, whether that be power, love, reassurance, stability...

And this is why I like to think of God as a Child, without that adult need to assert His intelligence, His identity. He is merely refreshingly present, unassuming; like something lying in your arms bringing comfort in whatever form you most need that to be.

So to get one step nearer that calm state in which you don't drop your bags, you don't panic, forget and stumble, listen quietly to your own choice of teachings. Listen, play, absorb, and watch them change into an energy that carries you safely through the crowd.

STEP SEVEN

COUNSELLING YOURSELF

Listen
don't comment
sit with me
and between us
the truth
will form
on the silence.

This morning, though alone in my room, I felt as if someone woke me up. I have been worrying about my job, more immediately fretting about the completion of my marking. There are a hundred and twenty exam papers to go. Yet this morning when I woke, it was as if someone was saying: 'I know; I know exactly what you're feeling; I know even more than you do, because I know how it will all turn out.' I got out of bed and sat in my wooden meditation chair. It is small, like something out of a nursery, and draws me into a childish pose immediately. As I sat, this feeling of being known flooded and quietened my mind.

It is very important to be known. It is very important, in the process of reconciliation with your own mind, to have a friend. A friend may say very little, but sitting in the room with you, his presence, like a healing crystal, can draw you into stillness. I think it was God this morning. God who has the knowledge of the past, the present, the future; God whose mantra says that everything that has happened is good, everything that is happening is very good, and whatever is going to happen will be very, very good. It was not me, for I was asleep. But in that accepting, knowledgeable presence was a lesson. It was as if - and this is why in reading this book, it does not matter too much whether you believe in God or not - that Being was demonstrating how one should be to oneself. One should be a friend.

A friend listens; a friend judges but not with hatred; has an opinion but is never acrimonious. No one wants a neutral, unthinking presence, but someone who puts ideas in a way that makes sense, who sets things to rest. A friend is not shocked, sees the best in you, talks it through.

The mind needs this steadiness, because it is subject to so many influences. It is subject to the influences of its own past, so that sometimes it feels one thing and sometimes, informed by a deeply buried experience, it feels another, as when I watched the court scene in 'Measure for Measure'. It is influenced by the messages sent by the senses and the messages sent to the senses by other people. It is so easily confused - it needs talking to and not always by a teacher, nor an over-concerned mother, nor a rigorous instructor, but an equal.

I remember, as a teenager at boarding school, going for weekends to Bournemouth. It was a strict school. The week was a busy schedule of work, more work, sport, team-spirited activities of every kind, by the end of which one felt more like a hockey stick than a person; an inanimate object swiping through life with too much force. Then on Friday night my friend and I were driven away by her father, down the long school drive, down those night-lit streets to the seaside. I can remember arriving in the dark hall, seeing the fire leap in the fireplace of her glass-partitioned sitting room. I can remember the joy of sleeping in a wide bed in a room of my own. I can remember the fragrance of clean sheets; towels that were soft, not pressed flat by an institutional laundry. I can remember tea not in a regulation mug but a cup and saucer, and best of all I remember the Saturday evening walk by the sea in the dark.

We would drive down to the beach and walk under the moonlight and the soft orange glimmer of old-fashioned street lights. And in those two hours strolling along the shingles to the sound of the waves, my friend and I shook away the formalities of school and spoke of the universe. Literally, school became as tiny as a star in the night sky. We spoke of our religious beliefs, our philosophy, our future, the books we were reading; and there was such joy because we were celebrating ourselves, our free thinking individual selves. This girl was my very best friend at that time. Because in her company I felt I shone, and so did she. We were growing up together.

The mind needs that kind of warmth as it grows up. It needs that secure framework in which to express what it is feeling. Often we look for that in other people. And if you find it in that way, you are lucky, for relationships in which true intimacy is possible are very valuable. But you are a very, very lucky person if you can give that friendship to yourself.

These days I often go for a walk alone. If I were to walk now with that school friend, there would be so much of each other we would not know, and maybe now that our lives have filled out and blossomed, we would not hear each other as clearly.

Walking alone I talk to my mind out loud. Yes, often out loud I conduct a question and answer session, particularly if I feel my mind shifting into a negative or unfamiliar key. I take it, so to speak, on an outing and I talk to it. And what stuns me again and again is how fast, how easily the mind becomes quiet; how, attended to in a mature way, it completely relaxes, and secondly, how wise that speaker is; how it seems to know what to say.

How can that be? How can it be that there is a persona inside us that knows the answers? I have come to believe that what people say about having your own angel is true. However, that angel is not a spirit guide from another astral plane, but your own accumulated and buried wisdom. It is a self which knows very well the truth of the matter, which is invisibly following your story and, when called upon to comment, does so calmly, because it is not suddenly introduced to the picture. It has always been there. It knows. Like God, it has stored within it the knowledge of the past and the future. It knows absolutely what is going to happen to you. Even if it does not have the most obvious access to that knowledge, that knowledge is there and the answers it will give you will spring from that knowing. They will be specific, often merely practical, but they will be based on an awareness of your destination. And it is for that reason that, in talking to yourself, you can draw your mind into silence. You can do it because the answers are authentic.

On those beach walks, my friend and I would often fall into silence, because we had reached a point where we were each satisfied. We had fed each other, we did not need more. And what is more, it did not matter if one of us was cross. The friendship was cemented too firmly for moods to break it. This girl was often very sullen; she was critical, melancholy, frequently sarcastic. She hated the pettiness of school. She was much more broad-minded than most of the teachers and indeed, I always thought, much cleverer. Sometimes I knew that she thought I was slow; she was irritated by my tendency to conform. But it did not matter; we were connected.

You are as connected - of course much more profoundly - to your own mind. It is a part of you, so rejection is a waste of time. Whatever your mind is doing, feeling, leading you to say, it is yours and you are stuck with it. No, not stuck, blessed. You cannot throw it away unless you destroy it with drugs or numb it with alcohol. And then, it will return to you even more difficult to deal with and resentful of your maltreatment.

Maybe you ask: 'But how do you know that the advice you give your own mind is right?' That is where teachings, beliefs and God come in. As teenagers, we needed each other because we were each other's protectors. If one of us was going too far, the other seemed naturally to stand in the way of danger and say: 'Hold on, don't go that way; that's a bit extreme.' Maybe we chose each other for that reason: I the conformist, she the rebel. We needed each other's perimeters. Now, I use belief; I use what I have come to understand and love about God.

God and the teachings I have come to associate with Him are now my reference point, my protection. For a politician that reference point will be party philosophy, for a priest his religion; for me, it is the teachings of Raja Yoga and through them what feels to be God's presence. I have consciously allowed them to colour, strengthen and divinise my intellect, precisely so that it can be a good friend, it can say the right words to my cavorting mind. And this is not brainwashing, for if it were, the mind would not quieten in the right way. It would be shocked and repressed into silence. But so many times I have felt a natural closing inwards, a natural slip into silence, that I have come to trust that with which I am shaping myself. It is a worthwhile aim to find such a framework and stick to it for a long time.

Raja Yoga says that the world of human souls is like a tree, that each soul is like a leaf and each leaf has its place on a branch. As the Buddhist writer Sogyal Rimpoche says, we are wrong to be suspicious of that potential for settledness, we are wrong to glorify doubt. There is a teaching to which your mind, that most difficult and truthful part of you, will respond. There is one road that is yours. It may be a life's work to find it, but it is there. Even to be looking is itself a destination, an acknowledgement of life's spiritual aspect. And when you do find it, you feel so comfortable that the prospect of further endless discoveries, which are refinements of that belief, only reinforces the security.

I feel that, as the drama of life draws to a conclusion, everyone will find their road. Somehow against all the odds, they will gravitate towards their pathway. And once on it, then they will begin to feel spacious inside, because they will feel tended to. Already it is happening. With a wonderful defiance of the cultures we were born into, Christians are becoming Buddhists, Buddhists Catholics, Christians Jews. We are all juggling around, because our souls are gravitating back to our roots, our original starting point. If you have not found that origin, you will. The right people will come, the right door will open, because it is the time for that.

I am thinking of my meditation chair again - hard-backed, small, comfortable. Why did I suddenly love it, though it was dragged out of the garden shed and put on the tip ready to be thrown away? Because, I think, it was a symbol of security, of having a special place in the scheme of things. Its back is crooked, its legs rock, but this morning, I felt that inner space that comes of being, however apparently oddly, in the right spot.

When you know your place, anyone who meets you will begin to find his place too because you are still. And that is the most dear and precious form of friendship you can offer anyone.

STEP EIGHT

SILENCE

My beginning
my end
my signal

All things faced
all souls loved
the self fully known

Home.

There is a state in which your mind is not only amenable to your intellect, that is, drawn by its friendship and wisdom into a state of contentment, but it is actually absorbed within it; it is inseparable. Not only your mind, but all that is of your past, having been attended to honestly, is folded away. You are one, whole integrated person, separate from your past, at a distance from your future, living naturally and yet righteously in the present. When you reach this stage, you have infinite space inside, because you are not cluttering yourself with anything unnecessary. You can have a foretaste of this closing into stillness in meditation. In moments, you can experience what we call the seed stage, in which you are completely without sense even of your own body. But to be that on a constant level, to really be it, you have to have dealt with yourself very lovingly, very thoroughly over a long period of time. It is as if then you have prepared for your death. You have walked the eight steps to silence.

First, you have accepted the fact that you are a child - however much in the world you are not. You have not rushed but allowed a mothering presence to set you off on your journey at the right time.

Second, you have systematically accustomed yourself to your naked, private, peaceful self. You have recognised and, in a sense, deadened - so that they feel like clothes merely: beautiful, colourful, various but inanimate - the roles that you play, the body that you live through, even the qualities you wield. And you have touched the peace that lies behind all of these. Again and again, in the quietness, you have sat with yourself, as before a guru, who accepts nothing less than the bare essence of yourself; the truth.

Third, you have recognised the need sometimes to be away from the ordinary. You have taken chances to be alone and acquainted yourself with the subtle dimensions of your commitments. You have allowed yourself to see why you are with who you are with, and begun to glimpse the intricacies of your mission, the form of your future; and been silenced by the excitement of that knowledge.

Fourth, you have learned to protect that specialness, to respect what seems to be mundane - your day-to-day life;

have pledged to banish the kind of hatred for life that destroys everything spiritual, everything healing; everything not just you, but the whole planet needs. You have learned, as from an extremely patient and appreciative teacher, to see that not an hour passes without something happening, however small, that can add to your wisdom.

Fifth, you have stayed with life, allowed yourself to be steered, as it were, by a Father figure into commitments and tasks that might at the outset have threatened to take your space completely. You have, with determined gentleness, taken out of those busy times moments for yourself, in which you have looked out onto a bigger universe.

Sixth, you have begun to realise how precious and vulnerable your mind is; and in seeing it as an infant, have focused more on it than on circumstance and so have become brave. For if you do not look again and again at circumstances, but instead at yourself, you cease to be frightened. In standing always face-to-face with yourself, a more impervious, stone-like part of you faces the world.

And penultimately you have learned the art of friendship, of celebrating the life of your own mind as you might the life and achievement of a friend. You have walked yourself through hardships, carefully explaining, supporting, coaxing, gently steering yourself away from extremisms. When all of that has become your practice, then it is possible for your mind to be drawn into your intellect like a child returning to the womb. You have attained simplicity.

The Romantics understood simplicity. They were also laughed at for it. Wordsworth was mocked when he wrote about little cottage girls and village idiots because, between the lines of those beautiful lyrics, lay the complications of his spirit. What appeared to be simple was not, because he was not.

Simplicity is an extremely elevated quality. It is the first stop and the last stop, to be experienced only by those in the pram and by people who have worked hard on themselves; if not in this life, in another. They are the people who see a rose as a rose, manure as manure, water as water. They can talk about good and evil with total equanimity, because in their soul is total knowledge and so detachment from both. As such, they are as close to God as any human person can be, because they have that same ease, that same concentrated full quality that comes of knowing, but having no need to exhibit their knowledge.

If you wish to become like this, again and again seek the company of God who is like that. Stand your consciousness next to His - meditate - and a power will absolve and return you to what **you** once were, before you expanded into expression.

Feeling that, and yet still living in a human body, you will not only be a person with inner space; you will be an angel...

CONCLUSION

Is it too much? Is it too much to begin with the notion of a comfortable journey on the Underground and end with angels? Maybe it is. But then inner space is a serious matter. It is also the most precious and special achievement a person can strive for.

I reassure you of one thing. At any point in a period of spiritual endeavour, you can experience space and stillness. Every time you realise a truth, every time you sense the hand of God in your life or the incidental support of a fellow traveller, you become mentally still. Every time you are blessed with an insight, see someone in a different light, understand why you are in the country you are in or the job, the family, the company... you become quiet.

What the mind responds to most is the truth. It will instantly silence when it hears the truth. And if ever you are not sure, listen to your body or look at your face in the mirror. Then you will see if you are lying or not.

I wish you luck and hope that, in whichever way you choose to find your peace, you enjoy it. Both the failures and the victories, though felt very deeply, are best regarded as moves in a game. A game in which not just you, but also nature, other people, negative and positive forces in the universe are the players. It is fascinating; it is fun; it is also a commitment.

Be light, be flexible - things pass - but also know one thing: that there is not infinite time for this process. One day it will be too late. Circumstances will close around us, so that there will not be the chance to fall down and get up with a mere laugh.

This time is very, very precious: not just because it is limited, but because it is blessed.

Other books to feed the soul

If you have enjoyed reading this book on Raja Yoga meditation as taught by the Brahma Kumaris World Spiritual University, you might like to read the following books to enhance your meditation practice and deepen your spiritual understanding.

Companion of God	Dadi Janki
Discover Inner Peace	Mike George
Eastern Thought for the Western Mind	Anthony Strano
Healing Heart and Soul	Roger Cole
In the Light of Meditation	Mike George
Inside Out	Dadi Janki
Pathways to Higher Consciousness	Ken O'Donnell
Practical Meditation	BK Jayanti
Restoring our Greatness	Dadi Janki
Soul Power	Nikki de Carteret
The Alpha Point	Anthony Strano
Touched by God	Jacqueline Berg

All the above books and a variety of meditation commentaries and meditation music are available from www.bkpublications.com

About the Brahma Kumaris World Spiritual University

The Brahma Kumaris World Spiritual University is an international organisation working at all levels of society for positive change. Established in 1937, the University now has over 8,000 centres in more than 90 countries. It actively participates in a wide range of educational programmes in areas such as youth, women, men, environment, peace, values, social development, education, health and human rights.

In 1996, the University's Academy for a Better World was opened in Mount Abu, India. The Academy offers individuals from all walks of life opportunities for life-long innovative learning. Residential programmes are centred on human, moral and spiritual values and principles. The University also supports the Global Hospital and Research Centre in Mount. Abu , India.

Local centres around the world provide courses and lectures in meditation and positive values, supporting individuals in recognising their own inherent qualities and abilities, and making the most of their lives.

All courses and activities are offered free of charge.

International Headquarters
Po Box No 2, Mount Abu 307501,
Rajasthan, India.
Tel: (+91) 2974-38261 to 68
Fax: (+91) 2974-38952
E-mail: abu@bkindia.com

International Co-Ordinating Office &
Regional Office For Europe And The Middle East
Global Co-operation House,
65-69 Pound Lane, London, NW10 2HH, UK
Tel: (+44) 208 727 3350
Fax: (+44) 208 727 3351
E-mail: london@bkwsu.com

REGIONAL OFFICES

Africa
Global Museum for a Better World,
Maua Close, off Parklands Road, Westlands,
PO Box 123, Sarit Centre, Nairobi, Kenya
Tel: (+254) 20-374 3572
Fax: (+254) 20-374 3885
E-mail: bkwsugm@holidaybazaar.com

Australia And South East Asia
78 Alt Street, Ashfield, Sydney, NSW 2131, Australia
Tel: (+61) 2 9716 7066
Fax: (+61) 2 9716 7795
E-mail: indra@brahmakumaris.com.au

The Americas And The Caribbean
Global Harmony House, 46 S. Middle Neck Road,
Great Neck, NY 11021, USA
Tel: (+1) 516 773 0971
Fax: (+1) 516 773 0976
E-mail: newyork@bkwsu.com

Russia, Cis And The Baltic Countries
2 Gospitalnaya Ploschad, Build. 1
Moscow - 111020, Russia
Tel: (+7) 095 263 02 47
Fax: (+7) 095 261 32 24
E-mail: bkwsu@mail.ru

http://www.bkwsu.org

Brahma Kumaris Publications
www.bkpublications.com
enquiries@bkpublications.com